Short Studies in Private International Law

Short Studies in Private International Law are short-book publications devoted to topics in private international law, in particular international and European civil procedure. The volumes can be a result of papers presented at conferences but can also consist of short monographs or edited volumes on private international law, aimed to inform academics and practitioners timely of recent developments. The hardcover books are compact volumes of 100–150 pages and are characterized by fast, global electronic dissemination, standard publishing contracts, standardized manuscript preparation and formatting guidelines, and expedited production schedules.

More information about this series at http://www.springer.com/series/15450

Christoph Schmon

The Interconnection of the EU Regulations Brussels I Recast and Rome I

Jurisdiction and Law

ASSER PRESS

Springer

Christoph Schmon
Nottingham, UK

ISSN 2522-8145 ISSN 2522-8153 (electronic)
Short Studies in Private International Law
ISBN 978-94-6265-366-5 ISBN 978-94-6265-367-2 (eBook)
https://doi.org/10.1007/978-94-6265-367-2

Published by T.M.C. ASSER PRESS, The Hague, The Netherlands www.asserpress.nl
Produced and distributed for T.M.C. ASSER PRESS by Springer-Verlag Berlin Heidelberg

This T.M.C. ASSER PRESS imprint is published by the registered company Springer-Verlag GmbH, DE part of Springer Nature.
The registered company address is: Heidelberger Platz 3, 14197 Berlin, Germany

Preface

The substantive scope and the provisions of this Regulation should be consistent with Council Regulation (EC) No 44/2001 of 22 December 2000 on jurisdiction and the recognition and enforcement of judgments in civil and commercial matters (Brussels I) and Regulation (EC) No 864/2007 of the European Parliament and of the Council of 11 July 2007 on the law applicable to non-contractual obligations (Rome II)—Recital 7 of the Rome I Regulation.

When interpreting EU private international law rules, the task of duly assigning the proper meaning to non-defined legal terms has proved tricky because the European Union may only legislate in specific areas and the set of European substantive law rules cannot yet provide for unified contract law concepts as a reference. Neither can the much-vaunted postulation of an 'autonomous' interpretation, an interpretation detached from meanings of a specific domestic law, be easily realised by a comparative approach. In many cases, there will be no *tertitum comparationis* that could serve as a comparative function. This suggests a systematic approach of interpretation to derive benefits from the reference points under the Treaties and to interpret the provisions of a legal act in due consideration of others. After all, every Union law provision must be seen in its context and interpreted in the light of the provisions of EU law and its principles.

A systematic approach would be particularly rewarding with respect to the key instruments of EU international contract law—the Regulations Brussels I Recast and Rome I. Whilst, due to various preliminary references since 1976, an abundance of case law exists with respect to the former and its predecessors, the contrary may be said for conflict of laws. Since it lacked jurisdiction for interpretation until 2004, the Court of Justice could not substantiate the terms of the Rome Convention and, consequently, the Rome I Regulation could not rely on rich case law or defined concepts. Both Regulations are historically and dogmatically connected and are embedded within the matrix of a judicial net of legislative acts of supranational character which pursue specific Union targets and serve as potential reference points for interpretation.

However, we have learned from comparative law that when words cross boundaries a morality is thereby attached to those words. Synergized legal terms require the conveyance of language and the legal culture those terms are stemming from. Something similar may be said when comparing these Regulations. Both legal acts have their specific DNA, system and underlying idea: Brussels I Recast has a procedural focus when it governs the allocation of jurisdiction and the free circulation of judgments. Rome I follows a conflict of laws rationale when it designates the law applicable to the contract. If one wishes to exploit synergy effects and to establish whether there can be a horizontal terminology across legal boundaries, it is necessary to delimit the scope and analyse the Regulations' systems, their individual justice models, internal and external target objectives, and their balance of flexibility and legal certainty. Such analysis is even more necessary as their legal DNA is encrypted by the value-laden authority of a *preludium*, the preamble of the legal text with its citations and recitals. Recitals intend to explain the text and to give the reasons on which the legal act is based. Sometimes though, they are programmatic or may even obscure the spiritual essence of the law. Recital 7 of the Rome I Regulation explains that its provisions should be consistent with those of the Brussels I and Rome II Regulations. Without doubt, it would be comforting if the same terms were presumed to bear the same meaning across the Regulations.

The mission of this book is thus to analyse the interconnection between the Brussels I Recast and Rome I Regulations and to address the questions of uniform interpretation and whether fragmentation may be avoided by way of systematic-teleological interpretation. Attention will be paid to the amalgamation of private international law on contractual obligations and Union law, taking into account the creation of an EU area of justice. Existing parallels and differences will be investigated, and the findings employed in the example of consumer contracts.[1]

Nottingham, UK Christoph Schmon

[1] Parts of this book build on the author's Ph.D.-thesis, submitted for approval in 2016 and successfully defended at the University of Vienna the following year. The author is grateful to the members of the doctoral committee and particularly wishes to thank those who encouraged him not to stop there but to go the extra mile.

Contents

Chapter 1
Complementarity

Contents

Abstract The Brussels I Recast and the Rome I Regulations are companions in a gradual unification process of private international law. Their predecessors already had a complementary function as the Rome Convention was created to thwart the tactical manoeuvre of forum shopping possible under the Brussels Convention. By embedding private international law matters in the corpus of Community law, the policy on judicial cooperation in civil matters strengthened their interrelationship even further. Keeping in mind the consistency of the unification process, the conventions were transformed into Regulations with modified content. Serving internal market purposes and being interlinked through a common Treaty competence, the Regulations serve as reference points of interpretation.

C. Schmon, *The Interconnection of the EU Regulations Brussels I Recast and Rome I*, Short Studies in Private International Law,
https://doi.org/10.1007/978-94-6265-367-2_1

Keywords Brussels Convention · Forum Shopping · Rome Convention · Treaty of Amsterdam · Brussels I Regulation · Rome I Regulation · Vertical Continuity · Court of Justice · Judicial Cooperation · EU Private International Law

1.1 The Age of Conventions

1.1.1 The Brussels Convention

The Convention on Jurisdiction and Enforcement of Judgments in Civil and Commercial Matters (Brussels Convention), signed on 27 September 1968 by the Members of the Community, was designed as a *convention double*: it not only established a system for recognition and enforcement of judgments, authentic instruments, and court settlements, as provided in Article 220 EEC, but also established an autonomous system of international jurisdiction in all Contracting States. The Convention superseded in its scope of application various bilateral conventions on jurisdictions and judgments concluded between the Contracting Parties (listed in Article 55 of the Convention). The Jenard Report explains that the 'differences between the bilateral conventions would hinder the 'free movement' of judgments'. The Report also states that the ideal solution would certainly have been to apply the Convention to all civil and commercial matters. However, a catalogue of exempted matters, such as matrimonial relationships or succession, was necessary in light of the difficulties resulting from the absence of any overall solution to the problem of conflict of laws.[1]

Consistent interpretation was to be ensured by the Luxembourg Protocol,[2] which awarded the European Court of Justice (ECJ)[3] the power of interpretation of the Treaty provisions when a reference would be made to it by a court of a Contracting State. The courts were thus compelled to follow the rulings of the Court of Justice when applying the Convention. As a result, the Luxembourg Protocol was heavily involved in making the resolutions of the Convention a 'successful model'.[4] The Convention came into force on 1 February 1973.

---

[1]Report on the Convention on jurisdiction and the enforcement of judgments in civil and commercial matters by Mr. P. Jenard [1979] C 59/1, 1, 7.

[2]Protocol Concerning the Interpretation by the Court of Justice of the Convention of 27 September 1968 on Jurisdiction and the Enforcement of Judgments in Civil and Commercial Matters, June 3, 1971 [1975] OJ L 204/28.

[3]Since the Lisbon Treaty, the Court of Justice of the European Union consists of the Court of Justice, the General Court (formerly the Court of First Instance) and specialised courts (formerly known as judicial panels). For the sake of clarity and ease of comprehension, the term 'Court of Justice' and the abbreviation 'CJEU' will be used throughout the present text to refer to the Court of Justice of the European Union.

[4]Geimer 2002, p. 33 (noting that one reason why the Hague conventions have not reached a greater expansion is the lack of central authoritative interpretation).

Its regime was—*cum grano salis*—extended to non-EU Member States with the Lugano Convention 1988,[5] concluded between the Member States of the European Community and certain Member States of the EFTA to facilitate closer co-operation. Other States could only accede with the unanimous approval of both the Community and the EFTA-States. In 2000, Poland received these approvals and acceded to the Lugano Convention. A protocol entrusting the Court of Justice to interpret the Convention was not adopted. The EFTA states could not have accepted referring the power of interpretation of a non-Community law legal act to an institution of the Communities,[6] nor had the EFTA States agreed to establish a genuine judicial body. Confronted with the 'complex situation' of guaranteeing uniform interpretation of the Lugano Convention and, at the same time, ensuring interpretation and application of the Convention in convergence with the Brussels Convention,[7] Protocol 2 and Declarations to the Convention were annexed. In essence, provisions of the Lugano Conventions were to be interpreted in light of the twin-provisions in the Brussels Convention and, therefore, the rulings of the Court of Justice had to be taken into account.

1.1.2 The Rome Convention

Since the Brussels Convention provided for the possibility of suing the defendant at different *fora*, the plaintiff could, by picking the most beneficial forum, choose the applicable law according to different national norms on the conflict of laws. The unified provisions of the Rome Convention were therefore created to thwart the tactical manoeuvre of 'forum shopping'.[8] On top of that, upcoming reforms in the Member States caused some to fear a danger that 'existing divergences would become more marked'. It was therefore regarded as a matter of urgency to continue cooperation in order to unify the Member States' rules on conflict of laws.[9] This was expressed by the Giuliano/Lagarde Report, accompanying the publication of the Rome Convention, which advised uniform conflict of laws norms in fields of particular economic importance in order to have the same law applied irrespective of the State in which the decision was rendered.[10] The collaborative function was explicitly exhibited by the Preamble of the Rome Convention, which explained that

---

[5]Lugano Convention of 1988 [1988] OJ L 319/9. For general comments, see Lechner and Mayr, *Das Übereinkommen von Lugano* (1996).

[6]Jenard and Müller-Report, Convention on jurisdiction and the enforcement of judgments in civil and commercial matters done at Lugano on 16 September 1988, [1988] OJ C 189/57 para 110.

[7]Id., para 111.

[8]For general thoughts on 'forum shopping', see Vareilles-Sommières 2007.

[9]Report on the Convention on the law applicable to contractual obligations by Mario Giuliano, Professor, University of Milan, and Paul Lagarde, Professor, University of Paris [1980] OJ C 282/1, 4.

[10]Id., p. 5.

the 'work of unification of law' commenced in the areas of jurisdiction and enforcement of judgments should be continued in private international law. It is worth noting that the initial proposal was addressed to bring a complete unification of the rules on conflict of laws 'over the whole field of private law':[11] the EEC preliminary draft convention[12] dealt with both contractual and non-contractual obligations. However, after the governments of the original and the new Member States[13] of the EEC re-examined the text, the expert group decided at its meeting in March 1978, 'for reasons of time' and in light of the enlargement of the EEC,[14] to restrict the scope of application of the Draft Convention to the field of contractual obligations, while the area of non-contractual obligations would be the subject of later legislative actions.[15] The Rome Convention was not formally based on Article 220 EEC but, instead, a result of the intergovernmental cooperation within the framework of traditional international law—civil cooperation outside of the legal order of the Treaty. A protocol conferring the jurisdiction of interpreting the Convention to the CJEU did not enter into force until 2004.

1.2 The Age of Regulations

1.2.1 An EC Policy on Judicial Cooperation

For decades, private international law and Community law had been considered separate areas, and initiatives had been solely taken by way of intergovernmental cooperation, as was the case with the Brussels and Rome Conventions. This changed with the coming into force of the Treaty of Amsterdam, which gave the starting signal for the harmonisation of private international law matters on a Community level. In contrast to the EEC Treaty of 1957, which did not explicitly mention private international law, the Amsterdam Treaty consolidated the areas of conflict of laws, jurisdiction, and the recognition and enforcement of foreign judgments, which comprised a new policy on judicial cooperation in civil matters. The embedding of private international law matters in the corpus of Community law resulted in adjustments to the traditional understanding of private international law. Community private international law had to serve the implementation of an internal market without frontiers and to meet the challenges brought by the process

[11]Minutes of the meeting of experts, cited in Id., at 4.

[12]Commission document, XIV/398/72. For a comprehensive commentary, see Foyer 1976, pp. 555–658; Lando/Hofmann/Siehr 1975; see also Czernich and Heiss 1999.

[13]Accession of the United Kingdom Denmark and Ireland to the EEC in 1973.

[14]Cf., however, Siehr 2000, p. 1358 (stating that the plan for a Convention on both contractual as well as non-contractual relations did not materialise because of the double actionability rule of *Phillips v Eyre*).

[15]Giuliano/Lagarde Report, n.9, p. 7.

of European integration.[16] For this purpose, private international law needed to be well-orchestrated. This was recognised in the 'Vienna Action Plan on how best to implement the provisions of the Treaty of Amsterdam', which emphasised the importance of creating private international law norms in such a way that their compatibility would be promoted.[17] In this context, it was recognised that the harmonisation of private international law would make a worthy contribution[18] to the functioning of the Internal Market, and it was also found that the risk of frictions among different legislative acts should be reduced by using a uniform terminology.

1.2.2 Brussels I Started, Rome I (II) Followed Suit

In order to implement the newly created Community policy on judicial cooperation, the Brussels Convention was transformed into the Brussels I Regulation with modified content. Consequently, the Rome Convention experienced a certain pressure to adapt, since the substantive revision of the Brussels Convention and the different institutional situation in which the legal acts were assembled complicated possible synergies. It was feared that the Rome Convention could no longer employ its supplementary function with full force. Certainly, that the Rome Convention was an international treaty outside of the Community order by no means disguises its strong connection, genetically and substantively, to the European Community. Although not adopted under Article 220 of the EEC Treaty, its preamble revealed that the Convention was a result of European legal harmonisation.[19] This connection was also emphasised by Article 28 of the Rome Convention stating that only EC Member States may be a party to it. The Contracting States thereupon adopted protocols allowing the Court of Justice to have exclusive jurisdiction to interpret the Convention.

---

[16] Kuipers 2012, p. 7 (noting that traditional PIL tries to serve international trade as a whole and not just the needs of intra-Union commerce); cf. Roth 1991, p. 638 (noting that already under the EEC Treaty, it was recognised that IPR may have an important role to play for the realisation of the four freedoms); Grundmann 2000, p. 458 (noting that EU private international law is remarkably different from classical PIL; noting on the Rome Convention, however, that it was a classical PIL act).

[17] Action Plan of the Council and the Commission on How Best to Implement the Provisions of the Treaty of Amsterdam on an Area of Freedom, Security and Justice [1999] OJ C 19/1, 15. Similar reflections are outlined in the conclusions of the Tampere summit and, building upon them, the agendas set out in the Mutual Recognition Programme and the Hague Programme.

[18] Meeusen 2004, pp. 43, 65.

[19] Preamble to the 1980 Rome Convention [1980] OJ 1989 L 266/1, 69: '[…] *to continue* in the field of private international law *the work of unification* of law which has already been done within the Community, in particular in the field of jurisdiction and enforcement of judgments, [and] to establish uniform rules concerning the law applicable to contractual obligations' (emphasis added).

The necessity for a substantive revision of the Rome Convention in accordance with the Brussels I Regulation and its transformation into a Community legal instrument was spelled out in the Green Paper on the Rome I Regulation in 2003 as well as in the Explanatory Memorandum to the Commission's Proposal for the Rome I Regulation. The latter referred *expressis verbis* to the Vienna Action Plan, the 2000 Mutual Recognition Programme, and the Hague Programme as 'grounds for the proposal'. The need for reform was ultimately met by the adoption of the Rome I Regulation in 2008.

1.2.3 The Recast Regulation

Article 73 of the Brussels I Regulation contained an obligation for the Commission to prepare a report no later than five years after the Regulation's entry into force. If so required, this report was to be accompanied by proposals for adaptations to the Regulation. The 'Heidelberg Report'[20] a study prepared for this reason by experts of European procedural law, provided a list of amendments. A Green Paper[21] published by the Commission in 2009 supplemented this report and initiated the consultation process. The most striking proposals concerned the abolition of the exequatur[22] procedure, the scope of jurisdiction with respect to nationals from non-Member States, the preconditions for prorogations of choice of court agreements, provisional measures, and the relation to procedures in arbitrary law.[23] On 14 December 2010, the Commission presented a proposal[24] for the reform,[25] accompanied by an Impact Assessment.[26] After years of debate, the revised Regulation 44/2001 was adopted in the official journal in the form of Regulation (EU) No 1215/2012.[27] The Recast Regulation, superseding Regulation 44/2001

[20]JLS/C4/2005/03 Report on the Application of Regulation Brussels I in the Member States (2007) 44.

[21]Green Paper on the review of Council Regulation No 44/2001 on Jurisdiction and the Recognition and Enforcement of Judgments in Civil and Commercial Matters, COM(2009) 175 final.

[22]On the Green Paper and for the function of exequatur, see Oberhammer 2010, p. 197.

[23]See Fucik et al. 2010; Mankowski 2010, p. 31.

[24]Proposal for a Regulation of the European Parliament and of the Council on Jurisdiction and the Recognition and Enforcement of Judgments in Civil and Commercial Matters, COM(2010) 748 final.

[25]See Hess 2011, p. 125.

[26]SEC (2010) 147 final.

[27]Regulation (EU) No 1215/2012 of the European Parliament and of the Council of 12 December 2012 on jurisdiction and the recognition and enforcement of judgments in civil and commercial matters [2012] OJ L 351/1.

(Article 80), entered into force on 10 January 2015. Although it incorporated many of the proposed changes,[28] it preserved the regime, system, and essential substance of its predecessor.

1.2.4 Review of the Rome I Regulation?

Likewise, the Rome I regulation contains a review clause on the evaluation of the Regulation. Article 27 obliges the Commission to carry out reports that include, if appropriate, proposals on the adaption of the Regulation by 17 June 2013. The review clause concerns the following matters: insurance and consumer contracts, assignments, and subrogation of a claim.[29] No report has been submitted to date and, for political reasons, a publication is not expected soon.

1.3 An Indissoluble Set of Private International Law Rules

1.3.1 Complementary Instruments

The Green Paper on the Rome I Regulation accentuated the unity of European procedural law and European private international law and urged the transformation of the Rome Convention into an instrument of Community policy in order to promote the consistency of the unification process.[30] The Paper went on to state that Brussels I, Rome I, and the future Rome II Regulations were considered 'complementary instruments'. It recalled the objective of the Rome Convention to 'ensure that the same solution will be applied as to the substance irrespective of the court hearing the case'. In view of the fact that the Convention only comprised contractual obligations, it stated that a future Rome II Regulation was a 'natural extension of the work on unifying the private international law rules on contractual and non-contractual obligations of a civil and commercial nature in the Community.'[31] The Green Paper explained that the conversion of the Convention into a Community instrument ensured that the Court of Justice would guarantee that

---

[28]For the changes and the legislative process, see Dickinson 2015, pp. 9–16.

[29]Heiss 2009, p. 217.

[30]Green Paper on the Conversion of the Rome Convention of 1980 on the Law Applicable to Contractual Obligations into a Community Instrument and its Modernization, COM(2002) 654 final, para 2.2. For more on this text, see Bonomi, 'Conversion of the Rome Convention on Contracts into an EC Instrument: Some Remarks on the Green Paper of the EC Commission' (2003) 5 YPIL 196.

[31]Green Paper on the Conversion of the Rome Convention of 1980 on the Law Applicable to Contractual Obligations into a Community Instrument and its Modernization, COM(2002) 654 final para 1.3.

'the legal concepts common to the Rome Convention and the Brussels I Regulation are interpreted in the same manner'. The Green Paper's stimulus to convert the Rome Convention into a (modernised) Community Regulation was strongly supported by the European Economic and Social Committee[32] and the European Parliament.[33]

By the same token, the Explanatory Memorandum to the Commission's Proposal underlined that the Rome Convention was the only Community private international law instrument that remained in international treaty form and that this was even less acceptable since the Brussels I, Rome II, and the Rome Convention Regulations should 'form an indissoluble set of Community rules of private international law'.[34]

1.3.2 Recital 7: Desire for Congruence

The legislative history and the legislator's intention are also summarised by the preambles of the Regulations. Recital 7 of the Rome I Regulation confirms the wish for a consistent interpretation.[35] Mirrored in Recital 7 of the Rome II Regulation, it explains that the substantive scope and the provisions of this Regulation should be 'consistent' with the Brussels I and Rome II Regulations.

The Regulations thus serve as reference points for interpretation. However, the desire for congruence does not necessarily lead to the congruence of concepts and provisions (the rationale will be discussed in Chap. 5). Neither should the authority of recitals be overestimated. They are intended to explain the operative text of an EU legal act or give the reasons on which the legal act is based (Article 296 TFEU (2)). They are thus important aids of construction and may help to identify the relevant objectives of the legal act. Nevertheless, caution should be exercised before predicating a proposition on the substance of recitals. As they do not form an operative body of the legislative act, Recitals do not constitute binding legal rules.[36]

---

[32]Opinion of the European Economic and Social Committee on the Green Paper on the conversion of the Rome Convention of 1980 on the 'Green Paper on the conversion of the Rome Convention of 1980 on the law applicable to contractual obligations into a Community instrument and its modernisation' (COM(2002) 654 final) [2004] OJ C 108/1.

[33]European Parliament Resolution on the prospects for approximating civil procedural law in the European Union (COM(2002) 654—COM(2002) 746—C5-0201/2003—2003/2087(INI)), A5-0041/2004.

[34]Proposal for a Regulation of the European Parliament and the Council on the law applicable to contractual obligations (Rome I) COM (2005) 650, 2.

[35]See also Leible 2009, p. 43; Bitter 2008, p. 96; Lein 2008, p. 177.

[36]Dickinson 2010, p. 125; Riesenhuber 2015, pp. 200–201.

They have no stand-alone 'operative effect'[37] and can never derogate an operative provision.[38] Their relevance may be unclear too: some recitals are mere standard boilerplates or programmatic rather than explanatory.

Recital 7 of the Rome I(II) Regulations seems to obscure rather than to illuminate the spiritual essence of the law. Interestingly, Recital 7 was replicated from the Rome II Regulation in the Rome I Regulation but not in the Brussels I Recast Regulation, post-dating the Rome Regulations. The preamble to the Recast Regulation only demands continuity with its predecessors, which were adopted before the Rome I Regulation. Indeed, the Brussels I Regulation served as a role model for the conceptualisation of legal terms in the Rome I Regulation, not vice versa.[39] Does this imply that the Rome I Regulation should be construed in light of the Brussels Regulation but not the other way around? After all, recitals may explain how to understand the operative text they accompany, however, they can hardly explain the provisions of another legal act. In this respect, Recital 7 may be very outspoken regarding a desire for coherence, yet, it does not spell out what 'consistency' means, and the phrasing indicates programme and intention, not necessarily obligation. Furthermore, Recital 7 is abstract and does not relate to specific provisions. Recital 17 of the Rome I Regulation, in contrast, explains *verbatim* that the concepts of 'provision of services' and 'sale of goods' should be interpreted in harmony with the corresponding concepts under Article 5 of the Brussels I Regulation. This example suggests that there is no *general* horizontal consistency between the Rome and the Brussels families but only 'where possible'. Why else should a Recital call for a uniform interpretation of a *specific* term? Such a specific call has also been made with respect to the concept of 'direct activity' as a condition for applying the consumer protection rules of the Recast and the Rome I Regulations, for which Recital 24 to Rome I explains that they must be 'interpreted harmoniously' for the sake of 'consistency' between the Regulations (discussed in Chaps. 4 and 8).

---

[37]Case C-308/97 *Manfredi v. Regione Puglia* [1998] ECR I-7685 [30] (recital cannot be relied upon to interpret provision in a manner clearly contrary to its wording); see also Case C-162/97 *Criminal proceedings against Nilsson and others* [1998] I-07477 (preamble has no binding legal force and cannot be relied on as a ground for derogating from the actual provisions of the act in question); Case C-215/88 *Casa Fleischhandels-GmbH v Bundesanstalt für landwirtschaftliche Marktordnung* [1989] ECR 2789 [31] (recital may cast light on the interpretation to be given to a legal rule, it cannot in itself constitute such a rule).

[38]Case C-134/08 *Hauptzollamt Bremen v J. E. Tyson Parketthandel GmbH* [2009] ECR I-2975 [16]: 'in that regard, it must be borne in mind, first, that the preamble to a Community act has no binding legal force and cannot be validly relied on either as a ground for derogating from the actual provisions of the act in question or for interpreting those provisions in a manner clearly contrary to their wording, see, *inter alia*, Case C-136/04 *Deutsches Milch-Kontor* [2005] ECR I–10095 [32] and the case-law cited.'

[39]Dickinson 2015, p. 28, para 1.77.

1.4 Vertical Continuity

1.4.1 General

In as much as the terminology has not changed and as long as there are no other reasons for a different interpretation,[40] such as the change of the underlying rationale, legal certainty suggests consistency of interpretation between the Regulations and their predecessors. The same logic applies for the Recast Regulation, the interpretation of which should refer to the *travaux préparatoires* to the 44/2001 Regulation.[41]

Article 80 of the Brussels I Recast Regulation demands the interpretation of references to the repealed Regulation as references to the Recast Regulation and, for this purpose, provides a correlation table in its Annex III. A similar statement is made by Article 68(2) as regards the Brussels Convention. Recital 34 explains the need for continuity between the Regulations and the 1968 Brussels Convention and stresses that the 'same applies' as regards the interpretation by the Court of Justice.

1.4.2 Court of Justice

'Vertical' continuity is also apparent in the rulings of the Court of Justice,[42] which refers to the former case law where the concepts remain the same.

> It should be borne in mind that, in so far as Regulation No 44/2001 replaces the Brussels Convention, the interpretation provided by the Court in respect of the provisions of that convention is also valid for those of the regulation whenever the provisions of those instruments may be regarded as equivalent [references to case law].

This statement, made by the Court of Justice in *Maletic v lastminute.com & TUI Österreich*,[43] affirms that the Court considers the EU Regulation Brussels I as a natural successor to the Convention, notwithstanding their different legal natures. On top of this, the Court has used the wording of an Article of the *ratione temporis* at the time of judgment, non-applicable Rome I Regulation to support the interpretation of the Rome Convention.[44] The fact that the CJEU principally interprets the Brussels and the Rome Convention according to EU legal

---

[40]Case C-533/07, *Falco Privatstiftung v Weller-Lindhorst* [2009] ECR I-3327 [48-50].

[41]Dickinson 2015, p. 27, para 1.73.

[42]C-419/11, ECLI:EU:C:2013:165, *Česká spořitelna, a.s. v Feichter*, 32-35; Case C478/12, Maletic v *lastminute.com GmbH* [2013] ECLI:EU:C:2013:735 [27]; Case C-147/12 *ÖFAB v Koot* [2013] EU:C:2013:490 [28]; Case 167/00, *Verein für Konsumenteninformation v Henkel* [2002] ECR I-8111 [49].

[43]Case C-478/12 *Maletic v lastminute.com Gmbh and TUI Österreich GmbH* [2013] ECLI:EU: C:2013:735 [27].

[44]Case 29/10, *Koelzsch v. État du Grand Duchy of Luxemburg*, [2011] ECR I-1595 [46].

methods[45] has consequences: neither the rules of interpretation contained in the Vienna Convention on the Law of Treaties nor those comprised in other international treaties can be used as a source of reference without further consideration. In line with the interpretation of international legal conventions, a legal-exegetical analysis of EU law will certainly use the classical methods of interpretation, taking into account the doctrines of uniform interpretation and *effet utile*. Nevertheless, specific doctrines of international law will not find application, such as the *dubio mitius* maxim, which serves infrequently as an interpretation aid for cases where the wording of a provision is unclear. Furthermore, the Treaties have assigned a far-reaching authority of jurisdiction to the Court of Justice, whose role is to ensure that the law is observed in the interpretation and application of the Treaties (the role of the Court of Justice will be discussed in Chap. 2).

1.4.3 Lugano Convention

With respect to the 2007 Lugano Convention, the context is given by a Protocol[46] on the uniform interpretation, stating that any court 'shall pay due account to the principles laid down by' the relevant decisions of national courts on the provisions in question of the 1988 Lugano Convention', the 1968 Brussels Convention, and the Brussels I Regulation (44/2001). An interpretative linkage is also established between the Lugano Conventions and the Brussels I Recast Regulation via its Article 80 ('[R]eferences to the repealed Regulation shall be construed as references to this Regulation').[47]

1.5 Conclusions

The Brussels I Recast and the Rome I Regulations are companions in a gradual unification process of private international law. Their predecessors already had a complementary function: As the Brussels Convention established an autonomous system of international jurisdiction with the possibility of forum shopping, the unified conflict of laws provisions of the Rome Convention were created to thwart this tactical manoeuvre. Their interrelationship was further strengthened by the policy on judicial cooperation in civil matters, which embedded private international law matters in the corpus of Community law. Having in mind the consistency

---

[45]As already mentioned, the first was formally based on Article 220 EEC whereas the latter is a classical international treaty created intergovernmentally outside of the EU legal order.

[46]Article 1(1) Protocol 2 on the uniform interpretation of the Convention and on the Standing Committee, L 339/27.

[47]Dickinson 2015, p. 27, para 1.74. On the Lugano Convention, see Dasser and Oberhammer 2008.

of the unification process, the conventions were transformed into Regulations with modified content.

Serving internal market purposes and being interlinked through a common Treaty competence, the Regulations serve as reference points for interpretation. The desire for complementarity is also expressed by the preambles of the Regulations, which call for a consistent interpretation. Vertical continuity allows interpretation of successive Regulations in congruence with previous case law.

References

Bitter A (2008) Auslegungszusammenhang zwischen Brüssel I-VO und Rom I-VO. IPRax 96-101

Bonomi A (2003) Conversion of the Rome Convention on Contracts into an EC Instrument: Some Remarks on the Green Paper of the EC Commission. YPIL 5:53–98

Czernich D, Heiss H (1999) EVÜ – Das Europäische Schuldvertragsübereinkommen. Orac Verlag, Vienna

Dasser F, Oberhammer P (2008) Kommentar zum Lugano Übereinkommen. Stämpfli Verlag, Bern

Dickinson A (2010) The Rome II Regulation – The Law Applicable to Non-Contractual Obligations. Oxford University Press, Oxford

Dickinson A (2015) Background and Introduction to the Regulation. In: Lein E, Dickinson A (eds) The Brussels I Recast Regulation. Oxford University Press, Oxford, 1.01–1.141

Fucik R and others (2010) Jahrbuch Zivilverfahrensrecht. Manz, Vienna

Geimer R (2002) The Brussels Convention - Successful Model and Old-Timer. EJLR 4:19–37

Grundmann S (2000) Binnenmarktkollisionsrecht – vom klassischen IPR zur Integrationsordnung. RabelsZ 64:457

Heiss H (2009) Party Autonomy. In: Ferrari F, Leible S (eds) Rome I Regulation: The Law Applicable to Contractual Obligations in Europe. Sellier European Law Publishers, Munich, pp 1–17

Hess B (2011) Die Reform der EuGVVO und die Zukunft des Europäischen Zivilprozessrechts. IPRax 125-130

Kuipers JJ (2012) Union law and Private International Law: The Interrelationship in Contractual Obligations. Martinus Nijhoff Publishers, Leiden

Lechner M, Mayr P (1996) Das Übereinkommen von Lugano. WUV-Univ.-Verlag, Vienna

Leible S (2009) Rom I und Rom II: Neue Perspektiven im Europäischen Kollisionsrecht. Schriftenreihe des Zentrums für Europäisches Wirtschaftsrecht 173:43–78

Lein E (2008) The New Rome I/Rome II/Brussels I Synergy. YPIL 10:177–198

Mankowski P (2010) Die Brüssel I-Verordnung vor der Reform. In: Verschraegen B (ed) 1 Interdisciplinary Studies of Comparative and Private International Law. Jan Sramek Verlag, Vienna, pp 31–79

Meeusen J (2004) Fifteen Theses on Brussels I, Rome I and the EU's Institutional Framework. In: Meeusen J and others (eds) Enforcement of International Contracts in the European Union. Intersentia Publishers, Antwerp, pp 43–76

Oberhammer P (2010) The Abolition of Exequatur. IPRax 197-203

Riesenhuber K (2015) Europäische Methodenlehre: Handbuch für Ausbildung und Praxis, 3rd edn. Beck, Berlin

Roth WH (1991) Einfluß des Europäischen Gemeinschaftsrecht auf das Internationale Privatrecht. RabelsZ 55:623–673

Siehr K (2000) Revolution and Evolution in Conflicts law. Louisiana Law Review 60:1353–1360

Vareilles-Sommières P (2007) Forum Shopping in the European Judicial Area. Hart Publishing, Oxford

Chapter 2
Reference Matrix of EU Law

Contents

Abstract The amalgamation of private international law and EU law has led to a firm systematic interconnection between the Brussels I Recast and Rome I Regulations. As law of the European Union, EU private international law follows, and must respect, the genuine principles and objectives of Union law. Both Regulations serve European integration and the implementation of the four freedoms. From an internal market perspective, the creation of an underpinning framework of coordinated rules on international jurisdiction, mutual recognition and enforcement of judgments, and harmonisation of laws and standards was inevitable. The Court of Justice is also a vehicle of EU integration and has helped to make early private international law a success. The Court has shown dedication to

C. Schmon, *The Interconnection of the EU Regulations Brussels I Recast and Rome I*, Short Studies in Private International Law,
https://doi.org/10.1007/978-94-6265-367-2_2

the Treaties and exercises an interpretation detached from national legal concepts. The aspiration for uniform, autonomous interpretation suggests a systematic approach of interpretation of the Brussels I Recast and the Rome I Regulations.

Keywords EU Private International Law · Harmonisation · Functional Integration · Internal Market · Governance · Court of Justice · Autonomous Interpretation · Legal Certainty · Four Freedoms

2.1 An EU Private International Law

2.1.1 Interconnection Through Harmonisation

EU private international law (PIL) did not have an easy start. Prior to the Amsterdam Treaty, the European Community was lacking in power to adopt uniform binding rules for all Member States, and thus, initiatives to unify private international law had primarily been taken on the intergovernmental level. A first attempt to bridge the legal gap between the national private international law systems and that of the European Union was made by the adoption of the 1968 Brussels Convention, based on Article 220 of the EEC Treaty, and with qualifications, the 1980 Rome Convention, to which only Member States of the EU could become party. Due to its legal nature, the Court of Justice had no power to interpret these international treaties and separate protocols had to be adopted to pave the way for uniform application.

The Treaty of Amsterdam changed this equation: with the aim of establishing a European Area of Justice, it reshaped and introduced judicial cooperation in civil matters into the Community sphere, entrusting the legislature with a broad private international law competence. Whether or not it was a good policy decision to place private international law matters right between the sensitive policies of visas, asylum, and immigration, the great achievement of the Amsterdam Treaty was that henceforth, Community law doctrines intertwined legal acts passed under Article 65 EC (now Article 81 TFEU), which thus formally took part in the integration process. A Community private international law had taken shape. At the same time, the Court of Justice was exclusively empowered to interpret and enhance Community private international law. With the entry into force of the Treaty of Lisbon, the integration process in the field of judicial cooperation culminated in the unification of the policy areas of justice and home affairs and the extension of the external dimension of the Area of Freedom, Security, and Justice (AFSJ) which advanced from a mere 'sub-concept for the implementation of an area of the Internal Market without border controls'[1] to an independent legal policy.

[1] [Integrationspolitisches Subkonzept zur Verwirklichung des binnenmarktlichen Raums ohne Binnenmarktgrenzkontrollen]. Müller-Graff 2005, p. 16.

The amalgamation of private international law and EU law has led to a firm systematic interconnection between related legal acts and has also brought changes for the method of interpretation. Harmonisation under the same competence norm resulted in the function of traditional PIL being extended to serve the implementation of the internal market and European integration. It is significant that after Article 65 EC was implemented and legislation in the realm of cooperation in civil matters was adopted, the demarcation line between PIL subject matters has often been drawn between those instruments rather than by reference to national law.[2]

The function of EU PIL to advance the goals of the internal market and to create a genuine intra-EU area of justice—as well as the option of the lawmaker to restrict the application or outcome of national conflict of laws rules and to advance mandatory EU rules—demonstrates that EU PIL is open to a neo-statutist approach. The Brussels I (Recast) and Rome I Regulations have become a supranational subject matter of an area that has at its core the cooperation of Member States of the European Union in civil matters and realisation of objectives as set out by the Treaties. As law of the European Union, EU private international law follows, and must respect, genuine EU principles and objectives. The need to judge and interpret rules on conflict of laws and jurisdictions in light of EU principles, in particular the four freedoms, has been demonstrated by the case law on international corporate law, restricting the application of the seat state's law.[3] The Europeanisation of the order public doctrine, the *Ingmar*[4] ruling, and the frontal attack of Savigny's PIL rationale in the form of EU law-protecting mandatory provisions are striking examples of the interrelation between EU law and private international law (the deviation of Savigny's ideal will be discussed in Chap. 5). It is also worth mentioning that the importance of access to justice was strengthened[5] for procedural matters in particular through the establishment of the Charter of Fundamental Rights,[6] acquiring primary law status.[7]

2.1.2 *Functional Integration*

The creation of EU private international law must therefore be understood in light of the process of functional integration, which has at its core the conferment of further assignments to the Union, and consequently, the enhancement of

---

[2]Cf. Study JLS/C4/2005/03 Report on the Application of Regulation Brussels I in the Member States by Hess and others (2007), 38.

[3]Case C-212/97 *Centros* [ECR] 1999 I-1459; Case C-208/00 *Überseering* [2002] ECR I-9919.

[4]Case C-381/98 [2000] ECR I-9305.

[5]TFEU Article 67(1) ('The Union shall constitute an area of freedom, security and justice with respect for fundamental rights and the different legal systems and traditions of the Member States').

[6]Charter of Fundamental Rights of the European Union [2000] OJ C 364/1.

[7]Reservations to the Charter were made by the British and the Polish governments.

competences.[8] The creation of an ever-closer union among the peoples of Europe also comprises the Area of Justice, which was first to be formed 'progressively' under the Amsterdam Treaty and later designated as a primary operative aim under the Lisbon Treaty. With regard to the judicial cooperation in civil matters, numerous legal instruments on judicial coordination, judicial cooperation, and conflict of laws were created to effectively facilitate access to justice for the citizens of the Union.

To avoid fragmentation of law and to guarantee its consistent application, EU regulations, directly effective in national systems, were chosen to form the legal corpus of Brussels I (Recast) and Rome I. The continuation of the process of EU integration in the Area of Justice is well described by the Regulation's recitals, which speak of a *gradual* establishment of an Area of Freedom, Security, and Justice through measures relating to the judicial cooperation in civil matters.[9]

2.1.3 The Internal Market Perspective

Although the Lisbon Treaty relaxed the links between the AFSJ and the Internal Market as the proper functioning of the latter was no longer a *sine qua non* for the adoption of measures under Article 81 TFEU, the progressive development of an Area of Justice certainly had a strong connection to the objective of creating an internal market without frontiers. This is stressed by the Regulation's recitals, which explain that the unification of private international law rules is necessary for the sound operation of the internal market and the predictability of the outcome of litigation.[10]

From an internal market perspective, the creation of an ever-closer union in the judicial area—based on mutual trust in the Member States' jurisdictional systems—was inevitable: The Community wished to create an internal market that facilitated the free movement of goods, services, capital, and people.[11] However, the disparities between the legal systems of the Member States are detrimental to these aims because they impede cross-border activities and cross-border-enforcement of legal decisions. This had been enforced by the increase of international trade, which called for uniform rules on private international law to promote certainty in transaction and law, as well as the protection of market participants and their equal treatment. Unification helps to reduce transaction and litigation costs, and ultimately decreases border effects, which disable the internal market from realising the endeavours set forth under primary law. What was consequently required was a correlating underpinning framework that coordinated national legal norms,

[8] Wolf 1992, p. 35.

[9] Recital 3 of the Brussels I Recast Regulation and Recital 1 of the Rome I Regulation.

[10] Recital 4 of the Brussels I Recast Regulation and Recital 6 of the Rome I Regulation.

[11] EC Treaty Article 3(c).

including flanking measures focusing on the allocation of jurisdiction, mutual recognition and enforcement, and harmonisation of laws and standards. For the area of conflict of laws, this was considered necessary as long as there is no uniform and comprehensive code on private law applying to all Member States.

2.1.4 Multi-level Governance

It is another feature of EU private international law that it must respect the transnational interests of the Member States and be sensitive to the evolution of EU private law. To some extent, its rules serve intra-Union trade and fulfil a certain 'constitutional function in multi-level governance'[12] because the question and need for harmonisation is linked to subsidiarity considerations. Where the European Union abstains from harmonising substantive law, EU private international law gains importance. Vice versa, PIL can be used to promote subsidiarity by giving order to the national private law systems. It can ensure the harmony of decisions without harmonising the substantive laws.[13] What can be sufficiently achieved or not by the Member States or what can be better achieved at Union level is not only a legal but also a political decision in a multi-level governance system about how close the ever-closer union should become. EU private law is a witness for a governance system that takes into account normative interests of their members when it focuses on incremental and targeted harmonisation of certain matters of concern, most importantly in the area of consumer protection, whilst preferring coordination rather than unification for most other matters. For this purpose, the TFEU gives broad power for coordinative measures in both internal and external matters. Regarding the latter, Recital 42 of the Rome I Regulation explains that only in exceptional cases should there remain a certain competence for Member States to negotiate and conclude agreements with third countries on their own behalf.[14] Another expression of a soft-touch approach is Recital 13, which anticipates the adoption of an optional contract law regime and explains that parties may choose to apply those rules. Mutual recognition—discussed below under the mutual confidence aspect—is another principle of coordination that pays respect to subsidiarity concerns. It disregards traditional conflict methodology in favour of an effective method to regulate the coexistence of different Member State orders.

In this context, Union-specific structural deficiencies can arise due to variable-geometry issues. Being at the crossroads between unity and flexibility, the

[12]Muir-Watt 2010, p. 49 (stating that, in contrast to the system of the United States, EU conflict of laws rules offer a means to avoid substantive unification).

[13]Kuipers 2012, p. 34.

[14]A procedure corresponding to this 'proposal' was established with the entry into force of Regulation 662/2009 on 13 July ([2009] OJ L 200/25). It authorises a Member State to amend an existing agreement or to negotiate and conclude a new agreement with a third country on particular matters concerning the law applicable to contractual and non-contractual obligations.

programmatic picture of an Area of Justice without frontiers is muddied by the exceptions granted to the United Kingdom,[15] Ireland, and Denmark, which geographically reduce the Area of Justice. This distortion is reinforced by the institutionalisation of enhanced cooperation mechanisms enabling a group of Member States to pursue their own agenda when creating PIL rules in their jurisdictions. Whilst enhanced cooperation 'shall not undermine the internal market' and shall neither 'constitute a barrier to or discrimination in trade between Member States [...] nor distort competition between them' (Article 326(2) TFEU, ex-Article 43 TEU (e-f)), it was, and still is, feared that such forms of variable-speed integration jeopardise the principles of legal certainty, predictability, and equal access to justice. It encourages 'forum shopping', and consequently also tests the much-vaunted credo of reciprocal confidence in the justice system of the Member States.

2.2 The Role of the EU Court of Justice

2.2.1 A Vehicle for Integration

Although the principles of subsidiarity and conferral are immanent barriers of interpretation, it is fair to say the Union law itself is used as a vehicle for EU integration. The EU treaties have assigned a far-reaching authority of jurisdiction to the Court of Justice, whose role is to ensure that the law is observed in the interpretation and application of the Treaties. Under the institutional provisions of Articles 19 TEU and 251 seqq. TFEU, legal development by criteria outside the realm of positive law is possible. The Court has consequently exercised 'judicial activism': particularly in times of legislative inactivity, it assumed responsibility to develop law rather than to merely give meaning to it or to close 'unintended gaps' in legislation. As regards private international law, the Court of Justice was awarded jurisdiction over the Brussels Convention as early as 1975 through the Luxembourg Protocol,[16] which consequently made the Convention a 'successful model'.[17] By contrast, a protocol conferring the jurisdiction to interpret the Rome Convention—which was not formally based on Article 220 EEC but, instead, a result of the intergovernmental cooperation within the frame of traditional international law—

[15] After the withdrawal of the United Kingdom from the European Union, the UK will lose the *ex-ante* and *ex post* opt-in possibilities under Title V of the TFEU. The Rome Regulations as well as the Brussels I Regulation will no longer apply.

[16] Protocol Concerning the Interpretation by the Court of Justice of the Convention of 27 September 1968 on Jurisdiction and the Enforcement of Judgments in Civil and Commercial Matters, June 3, 1971 [1975] OJ L 204/28.

[17] Geimer 2002, p. 33; cf. Kerameus 2002, p. 12 (noting that one reason why the Hague conventions have not reached a greater expansion is the lack of central authoritative interpretation).

did not enter into force until 2004. Not until another five further years had passed could the Court of Justice rule on its first judgment.

2.2.2 *More Competences*

The process of 'communitarisation' of private international law by the Treaty of Amsterdam and the establishment of the Area of Justice as an independent EU policy in the Lisbon era further strengthened the position of the Court. It was assigned general judicial competence to ensure coherence of EU law by interpreting EU private international law. Since the entry into force of the Lisbon Treaty, subject matters of the Area of Freedom, Security, and Justice are substantially supranational under the general jurisdiction of the Court of Justice, and references for a preliminary ruling can be requested by all national courts and tribunals under Article 267 TFEU. As the Brussels I Recast and Rome I Regulations are EU legislation, they must be construed in the light of the objectives set out in the Treaties and the general principles developed by the Court of Justice. Some of the relevant principles for the application of PIL shall be discussed below, others where appropriate.

2.3 Selected Principles of Union Law

2.3.1 *Duty of Sincere Co-operation*

An important example of a Treaty-based principle is the duty of sincere co-operation as set out in Article 4 of the European Treaty:

> The Union and the Member States shall, in full mutual respect, assist each other in carrying out tasks which flow from the Treaties. The Member States shall take any appropriate measure, general or particular, to ensure fulfilment of the obligations arising out of the Treaties or resulting from the acts of the institutions of the Union. The Member States shall facilitate the achievement of the Union's tasks and refrain from any measure which could jeopardise the attainment of the Union's objectives.

The duty of loyal cooperation has undergone a remarkable evolution in past decades and is now considered 'a multi-sided duty of loyalty and good faith in the vertical relationship between the Union and its Member States and also among the Member States themselves and among the Union institutes.'[18] Embodied in Articles 4(3), 13(2), and 24(3) TEU, the principle of loyalty obliges the Member States to promote the objectives of Union law and to take all necessary measures to guarantee its effectiveness. It imposes duties of cooperation on the Member States

[18] Curting and Dekker 2002, pp. 63–64.

as well as the Union institutions.[19] Article 7 TFEU clarifies that 'the Union shall ensure consistency between its policies and activities, taking all of its objectives into account and in accordance with the principle of conferral of powers'. The *effet utile* doctrine is embodied in it. With respect to EU PIL, it requires giving useful effect to any Union law rule and interpreting a legislative rule in view of the Union's objective to create an effective Area of Justice, thereby serving the goal of further integration.[20]

The Court of Justice has regularly relied, at least indirectly, on this principle. In *Francovich*,[21] the Court referred to the necessity of full effectiveness of Community rules and held that individuals must be able to obtain compensation when their rights are infringed by a breach of Community law for which a Member State can be held responsible. The importance of full effectiveness of PIL Community rules was demonstrated in the case *Allianz SpA v West Tankers*, where a Member State's court issued an injunction that restrained a party from commencing or continuing proceedings in another Member State on the grounds that such proceedings were in breach of an arbitration agreement. Although arbitration is excluded from the scope of the (recast) Brussels I Regulation, the Court of Justice ruled that its effectiveness would nevertheless be undermined where such court orders would 'prevent a Member State from exercising the jurisdiction conferred on it by the Regulation'.[22]

With respect to Article 9(3) of the Rome I Regulation,[23] it is considered that the principle of loyal cooperation could require Member States to give effect to the overriding mandatory provisions of another Member State where this may otherwise result in 'unnecessary or unjustifiable harm' for this Member State.[24]

2.3.2 *Mutual Confidence*

Another basic principle of Union law closely connected with that of sincere cooperation[25] is that of mutual confidence. Trust in the Member States' judicial systems is considered the 'bedrock upon which EU justice policy should be

[19]Case 2/99 *Zwartveld* [1990] ECR I-3365.

[20]See Magnus and Mankowski 2007, p. 37.

[21]Joined Cases C-6/90 and C-9/90 [1991] ECR I-5357.

[22]Case C-185/07 *Allianz SpA v West Tankers Inc* [2009] ECR I-663. For arbitral injunctions and the relationship to the Brussels I Recast Regulation, see Regulation, Schmon 2015, 669.

[23]This provision allows effect to be given 'to the overriding mandatory provisions of the law of the country where the obligations arising out of the contract have to be or have been performed, in so far as those overriding mandatory provisions render the performance of the contract unlawful'.

[24]Lang 1999, p. 677; Sonnenberger 2006, p. 116 (stating that, insofar as there is a community duty, 'may must be read as must').

[25]Dickinson and Lein 2015, p. 25, para 1.68 (considering the principle of mutual trust as but one facet of the principle of sincere cooperation).

built'[26] and it forged the development of EU private international law. The crucial goal, as formulated by the Conclusions of Tampere[27] and the Mutual Recognition Programme,[28] was to create a genuine European Area of Justice, where legal decisions are free to circulate without restraint. Hence, the 'country of origin-principle' attained substantial importance. This principle, initially aimed at avoiding the detrimental effects of diverse national product standards, came in the form of the 'principle of mutual recognition':[29] the effects that a legal judgment has in its state of origin should be recognised without restriction in the European Union. The declaration of enforceability, the 'exequatur,' was to be abolished. This was also meant to have the positive side-effects of facilitating co-operation between authorities and better judicial protection of individual rights. Mutual recognition was progressively formed as an institutional conflict mechanism, as demonstrated by the joint cases *Gözütok* and *Brügge*, where the CJEU gave weight to the concept of mutual trust when ruling on the application of the *ne bis in idem* principle in criminal matters. The Court of Justice underlined the importance that the Member States recognise criminal law in force in the other Member States 'even when the outcome would be different if its own national law were applied.'[30]

The principle of mutual trust was implemented by the Brussels I (Recast) Regulation, which abolished, save for some minor exceptions, restrictions to the free movement of judgments. The Court of Justice referred to it on several occasions when it found that the compulsory system of jurisdiction and that of recognition and enforcement of judgment was based on 'the trust which the Contracting States accord to one another's legal systems and judicial institutions'[31] or when it concluded that a review of the international jurisdiction of a national court should only take place in 'exceptional cases'.[32] The duty to recognise a decision without possibility of corrective or supervisory measures also means that Member States potentially compete with each other as 'law providers' if the law on jurisdiction permits a multiplicity of jurisdictional grounds. The resulting disharmonious decisions and the attractiveness of 'forum shopping' could then undermine

[26]Commission's Communication, The EU Justice Agenda for 2020—Strengthening Trust, Mobility and Growth within the Union, COM(2014)144 final.

[27]Conclusions of the Presidency of the European Council [1999] 10 Bulletin of the European Union.

[28]Draft Programme of Measures for Implementation of the Principle of Mutual Recognition of Decisions in Civil and Commercial Matters [2001] OJ C 12/1 (Mutual Recognition Programme).

[29]Mansel 2006, p. 651. On the principle of mutual recognition in private international law, see Rieks 2012; see also the Communication from the Commission to the Council and the European Parliament on 'Mutual Recognition of Final Decisions in Criminal Matters COM(2000) 495 final, according to which mutual trust would be 'an important element, not only trust in the adequacy of one's partners' rules, but also trust that these rules are correctly applied'.

[30]Joint Cases C-187/01 and C-385/01 *Gözütok and* Brügge [2003] ECR I-1345.

[31]Case C-159/02 *Turner v Grovit* et al. [2004] ECR I- 3565 [24].

[32]Case C-351/89 *Overseas Union Insurance Ltd* [1991] ECR I-3317.

reciprocal confidence in the legal systems. From this perspective, the harmonisation of conflict of laws has a strong connection to the mutual recognition programme. In order to avoid distortions of competition and to meet the standards of legal certainty and predictability, it would also be conceivable to implement a system in which recognition and enforcement procedures are accompanied by a regime of exclusive grounds for jurisdictions. Such a system, however, could hardly satisfy procedural purposes, nor could it prevent courts from succumbing to the temptation of applying the *lex fori* whether or not the case had a cross-border dimension or would be the proper law.

That being said, to uplift mutual trust from a programmatic idea to a somewhat axiomatic[33] procedural principle comes at a price. Should a foreign judgment be blindly accepted and enforced at will of the creditor even if it was issued by courts of judicial systems that may not have improved to the point where it is safe to assume it would always offer adequate protection of the debtor? The question of procedural fairness and access to justice cannot be put aside by a statistical argument that appeals have rarely been brought in practice. It is the essence of judicial or administrative control to be fit for exceptional cases. It was therefore a relief for many that the Brussels I Recast Regulation has not abandoned the public policy exception (*ordre public*), as initially envisaged by the Commission, and allows the debtor to apply for refusal of enforcement for important grounds.[34]

2.3.3 Autonomous Interpretation

To ensure the effectiveness of EU law, the Court of Justice has made it a well-established principle that legal terms should normally be given an independent and uniform interpretation throughout the Union.

In *Finanzamt Rendsbug v Detlev Harbs*, the Court held that (emphasis added):

> It should also be observed that, in determining the scope of a provision of Community law, its wording, context and objectives must all be taken into account [References to case law]. Moreover, *the need for uniform application of Community law and the principle of equality require that the terms of a provision of Community law which makes no express reference to the law of the Member States for the purpose of determining its meaning and scope must normally be given an autonomous and uniform interpretation throughout the Community*; that interpretation must take into account the context of the provision and the purpose of the legislation in question [References to case law].[35]

[33]Oberhammer 2010, p. 72 (speaking of 'integration dogmatism').

[34]Thöne 2015, p. 149; Frauenberger-Pfeiler 2014, p. 24.

[35]Case C-321/02 [2004] ECR I-7101, para 28. For a general view, see Riesenhuber 2015, p. 201.

The same was spelled out on many occasions as regards private international law rules.[36] When the Court of Justice breathed life into the provisions of the Brussels Convention—which it interpreted according to EU law methods—it stressed the importance to 'guarantee the harmonious operation of expressions and concepts allied to the Community order.'[37] It was therefore necessary to interpret concepts which may have different content in the Contracting stats, independently 'in order to ensure that the Convention is uniformly applied in all the Contracting States.'[38] Save for some exceptions,[39] the Court will therefore not shape concepts by redressing to a specific national law but mainly by referring to the legislative act itself or related legal acts.

The desire for uniform, autonomous interpretation can unquestionably also be found in the sphere of international unified law, where the drafters of conventions make use of an arsenal of options to prevent re-nationalisation. The CISG and the Rome Convention provide explicit provisions that regard should be given to their international character and to the desirability of achieving uniformity. In the case of the Rome Convention, a protocol conferring the jurisdiction to the Court of Justice underlined the importance of uniformity, to which the contracting parties jointly declared to be 'anxious to prevent differences of interpretation of the Convention from impairing its unifying effect'. However, the autonomous interpretation under EU law will be exercised according to EU methods, hence an interpretation mindful of the integration process and abstaining from restrictively construing ambiguous terms in light of state sovereignties involved. An EU autonomous interpretation requires accepting the reference points of and under the Treaties, such as the Area of Justice objectives, the four freedoms, or fundamental rights, even more so as these reference points had been the starting-point for drafting the legal acts in the first place. It will also take related legal acts into account. The impact of communitarisation on the method of interpretation can be illustrated on the example of the case *Leffler*,[40] in which the Court laid down not only the importance of the effectiveness of Union law but also the requirement to interpret it dynamically[41] by taking into account the progressive integration of the European Union (emphasis added):

---

[36]For example, Case C-360/12, *Coty Germany GmbH v First Note Perfumes NV* [2014] ECLI:EU:C:2014:1318 [43]; Case C-228/11 *Melzer* EU:C:2013:305 [22]; Case C-189/08, *Zuid-Chemie BV* [2009] ECLI:EU:C:2009:475 [17]; see with respect to the Rome II Regulation Case C-189/87 [1998] ECR 5565, *Kalfelis v Bankhaus Schröder* [15-16].

[37]Case 150/77, *Bertrand v Paul Ott KG* [1978] ECR I-1431 [15-16].

[38]Case C-89/91 *Shearson Lehmann Hutton Inc. v. TVB Treuhandgesellschaft für Vermögensverwaltung und Beteiligungen mbH* [1993] ECR I-139 [13].

[39]For example, the last sentence of Article 24(2) Brussels I Recast Regulation: [...] In order to determine that seat, the court shall apply its rules of private international law; see also Recital 27 of the Rome II Regulation: "The exact concept of industrial action, such as strike action or lock-out, varies from one Member State to another and is governed by each Member State's internal rules".

[40]Case C-443/03 *Leffler v Berlin Chemie AG* [2005] I-9611 [43-45].

[41]Hess 2006, p. 358.

> This interpretation cannot be successfully countered by the submission that the consequences of refusal of a document should be determined by national law. The comments in the explanatory report on the Convention, the Court's decision in Lancray, cited above, and the Regulation's drafting history *cannot properly be relied upon in this connection* (43).
>
> The *objective pursued by the Treaty of Amsterdam* of creating an area of freedom, security and justice, thereby giving the Community a new dimension, and the *transfer from the EU Treaty to the EC Treaty of the body of rules enabling measures in the field of judicial cooperation in civil matters* having cross-border implications to be adopted testify to the will of the Member States to establish such measures firmly in the Community legal order and thus to lay down the principle that they are to be *interpreted autonomously* (45).

2.3.4 Due Consideration of Related Legal Acts

The task of independently assigning the proper meaning to non-defined legal terms proves tricky where the necessary conceptualisations or legal definitions are missing. In many cases, an 'autonomous' interpretation may also not be realised by a comparative approach. In many cases, there will be no *tertitum comparationis* that could serve as a comparative function. Even a comparative approach attentive to the constitutional and cultural pluralism of the Member States will often produce lowest common denominators rather than what GA Lagrange boldly assumed as being in line with the spirit of the Court, 'solutions which, having regard to the objects of the Treaty, appear to it to be the best [...]'.[42] Particularly in the infancy of the Brussels Convention, the Court of Justice referred explicitly to general principles stemming

[42]Case C-14/61 *Hoogovens v High Authority* [1962] ECR 485, Opinion of Advocate-General Lagrange, 283–284. It should be noted, however, that the significance of comparative law is beyond doubt. The comparative method is of utmost importance for both the development and the application of private international law. Both disciplines deal with foreign law and have, *inter alia*, international collaboration in matters of private justice in mind. Proof of their interaction can be found on academic, legislative, and judicial levels. Comparative law supplements private international law, and the latter may sometimes even depend on the first, see von Bar 1987, p. 6; for a general view, see id., pp. 92–98. Nevertheless, due to the rise of a new *ius commune*, the importance and use of the comparative method largely differs according to the subject matter. The higher the degree of uniformity in private law (often accomplished with the comparative method), the more private international law will become somewhat 'superfluous', see Reimann 2012, p. 17. For the challenges of comparative law with respect to the unification of private law in the European Union, see Zimmermann 2006. For a general introduction into the studies of comparative law, see, e.g., Gutteridge 1971. For the question of whether the comparative method can contribute to the development of (public) Union law, see Legrand 2002, p. 225 (thoughtfully explaining the challenges and criticism of comparative law and pointing out the necessity to 'move away from hubristic programmes engendering a frenetic and hasty search for commonalities which-clearly-must-be-there-since-we-want-them-there' and claiming that 'meaningful comparative work demand [...] individuals who accept that [...] [an] understanding of law or of an experience of law other than one's own can only arise from thorough cultural contextualisation'). For the importance, deduction, and application of general principles in European private law, see Metzger 2009.

'from the corpus of the national legal systems'[43] to give shape to legal concepts. However, where this was not of assistance and in the absence of legal development, such as in the famous *Tessili* case in which the Court faced the problem of not being able to give substantial guide to the interpretation of the 'place of performance' under Article 5(1), the Court referred to national laws.[44]

An EU autonomous interpretation also suggests paying specific attention to related legal acts. A systematic approach of interpretation would indeed be particularly rewarding with respect to the Regulations Brussels I Recast and Rome I. Whilst, due to various preliminary references since 1976, an abundance of case law exists with respect to the former and its predecessors, the contrary may be said for conflict of laws. Since it lacked jurisdiction for interpretation until 2004, the Court of Justice could not substantiate the terms of the Rome Convention and the Rome I Regulation could not rely on rich case law or defined concepts.

2.3.5 Legal Certainty

The principle of legal certainty is considered 'part of the legal order'[45] of the European Union and has been increasingly applied by the Court of Justice, which identified the protection of legitimate expectations as a fundamental principle and held that 'legislation must be unequivocal and its application must be predictable for those who are subject to it'.[46] In this sense, and with a look at legal reasoning, it can be concluded that legal certainty 'favours the equality and uniformity across the Member States of rights and obligations arising from the Regulations, and favours respect for the wording and scheme of the Regulations'.[47] Recital 9 of the Rome III Regulation[48] states that the Regulation should create a clear, comprehensive legal framework and emphasises the importance of legal certainty and predictability (as well as flexibility). Similarly, the Brussels I and Rome I Regulations designate legal certainty as one of their general objectives and argue in favour of highly foreseeable rules. This is reflected by the rules on party autonomy, which promote legal certainty in that the parties themselves, save for some exceptions, are free to determine the competent forum and the applicable law at the very outset of their contractual relationship (Article 3 Rome I, Article 25 Brussels I Recast). Leading

---

[43]Case 29-76 *LTU Lufttransportunternehmen GmbH & Co. KG v Eurocontrol* [3].

[44]Case 12/76 *Industrie Tessili Italiana Como v Dunlop AG* [1976] ECR 1473 [9].

[45]Cases 205-215/82 *Deutsche MilchKontor GmbH v Germany* [1983] ECR 2633.

[46]Case 70/83 *Kloppenburg v Finanzamt Leer* [1984] ECR 01075 [11].

[47]Briggs 2014, p. 55, para 2.46; Case 169/80 *Gonrdrand*, [1981] ECR 1931.

[48]Council Regulation No 1259/2010 of 20 December 2010 implementing enhanced cooperation in the area of the law applicable to divorce and legal separation [2010] L 343/10.

decisions of the Court of Justice have stressed the importance of legal certainty with respect to international jurisdiction in particular. Legal certainty calls for a uniform application and interpretation of Union law, thereby advocating that both relevant legal acts and the Court's case law be taken into account.

2.4 Conclusions

The amalgamation of private international law and EU law has led to a firm systematic interconnection between the Brussels I Recast and Rome I Regulations and has also brought changes in methods of interpretation. Harmonisation under the same competence norm resulted in the function of traditional PIL being extended to serve European integration. As law of the European Union, EU private international law follows, and must respect, the genuine principles and objectives of Union law. Both Regulations serve European integration and the implementation of the four freedoms and their design show that they are open to a neo-statutist approach. The creation of an underpinning framework of coordinated rules on international jurisdiction, mutual recognition and enforcement of judgments, and harmonisation of laws and standards was inevitable to advance the goals of the internal market. Also, as EU law, EU private international law respects the transnational interests of the Member States and is sensitive to the evolution of EU private law.

The Court of Justice is a vehicle of EU integration as well and has helped to make early private international law a success. The Court showed dedication to the Treaties and exercised an interpretation detached from national legal concepts. The desire for uniform, autonomous interpretation demands a systematic approach of interpretation of the Brussels I Recast and the Rome I Regulations.

References

Briggs A (2014) Private International Law in English Courts. Oxford University Press, Oxford

Curting D, Dekker I (2002) The Constitutional Structure of the European Union: Some Reflections on Vertical Unity-in-Diversity. In: Beaumont B, Lyons C, Walker N (eds) Convergence and Divergence in European Public Law. Oxford University Press, Oxford, pp 59–78

Dickinson A, Lein E (2015) The Brussels I Regulation Recast. Oxford University Press, New York

Frauenberger-Pfeiler U (2014) EuGVVO "2.0" in Kraft - Änderungen bei Anerkennung und Vollstreckung. JAP 24:240–243

Geimer R (2002) The Brussels Convention - Successful Model and Old-Timer. EJLR 4:19–37

Gutteridge HC (1971) Comparative law: An Introduction to the Comparative Method of Legal Studies, Comparative law and the Conflict of Laws. Cambridge University Press Archive, Cambridge

Hess B (2006) Methoden der Rechtsfindung im Europäischen Zivilprozessrecht. IPRax 348-363

Kerameus KD (2002) Angleichung des Zivilprozeßrechts in Europa: Einige Grundlegende Aspekte. RabelsZ 66:17

Kuipers JJ (2012) EU Law and Private International Law: The Interrelationship in Contractual Obligations. Martinus Nijhoff Publishers, Leiden

Lang JT (1999) Community Constitutional Law: Article 5 EEC Treaty. CMLRev 27:645–681

Legrand P (2002) Public Law, Europeanisation, and Convergence: Can Comparatists Contribute? In: Beaumont P and others (eds) Convergence and Divergence in European Public Law. Hart Publishing, Oxford-Portland Oregon, pp 225–256

Magnus U, Mankowski P (2007) Brussels I Regulation: European Commentaries on Private International Law. Sellier European Law Publishers, Munich

Mansel HP (2006) Anerkennung als Grundprinzip des europäischen Rechtsraums. RabelsZ 70:651–731

Metzger A (2009) Extra legem - intra ius: Allgemeine Rechtsgrundsätze im Europäischen Privatrecht. Mohr Siebeck, Tübingen

Muir-Watt H (2010) The role of conflict of laws in European private law. In: Twigg-Flesner C (ed) European Union Private Law. Cambridge University Press, Cambridge, pp 44–57

Müller-Graff PC (2005) Der Raum der Freiheit, der Sicherheit und des Rechts. Nomos, Baden-Baden

Oberhammer P (2010) Freier Urteilsverkehr durch Abschaffung des Vollstreckbarerklärungsverfahrens und der Anerkennungsversagungsgründe. In: Fucik, Konecny and others (eds) Jahrbuch Zivilverfahrensrecht. Manz, Vienna, pp 69–78

Reimann M (2012) Comparative Law and Neighbouring Disciplines. In: Bussani M, Mattei U (eds) The Cambridge Companion to Comparative Law. Cambridge University Press, Cambridge, pp 13–34

Rieks J (2012) Anerkennung im Internationalen Privatrecht. Nomos, Baden-Baden

Riesenhuber K (2015) Europäische Methodenlehre: Handbuch für Ausbildung und Praxis, 3rd edn. Beck, Berlin

Schmon C (2015) EuGVVO auf Frage der Anerkennung einer anti-suit injunction durch ein Schiedsgericht nicht anwendbar. ecolex 669

Sonnenberger HJ (2006) Internationales Privatrecht, Einl. IPR. In: Sonnenberger HJ (ed) Münchener Kommentar zum BGB, 4th edn. 10 Internationales Privatrecht, C.H. Beck, Munich, pp 5–365

Thöne M (2015) Der Abschied vom Exequatur. GPR 149-154

Von Bar C (1987) Internationales Privatrecht, I Allgemeine Lehren. Beck, Munich

Wolf M (1992) Abbau prozessualer Schranken im europäischen Binnenmarkt. In: Grunsky W and others (eds) Wege zu einem europäischen Zivilprozessrecht. Mohr Siebeck, Tübingen, pp 35–69

Zimmermann R (2006) Comparative Law and the Europeanization of Private Law. In: Reimann M, Zimmermann R (eds) The Oxford Handbook of Comparative Law. Oxford University Press, Oxford, pp 539–577

Chapter 3
System and Scope

Contents

Abstract The Brussels I Recast and the Rome I Regulations show certain systematic commonalities, such as the idea of proximity to the dispute or legal relationship or that they set out a rule-exception relation between general and special rules. Leaving this aside, there are many infrastructure differences. The Brussels I Recast Regulation is driven by the goal of providing access to the courts of the EU Member State where the defendant is domiciled. Compensation for this jurisdictional preference is provided by special grounds for jurisdiction that focus on the subject-matter in dispute. The Rome I Regulation, by contrast, cannot be concerned

C. Schmon, *The Interconnection of the EU Regulations Brussels I Recast and Rome I*, Short Studies in Private International Law,
https://doi.org/10.1007/978-94-6265-367-2_3

with such jurisdictional thoughts. Its general rules do not generally protect one party to the contract and its formula gives a strong priority to party autonomy. There is thus no parallel feature to 'general jurisdiction' in conflict of laws, as a default rule would thwart its idea of qualification. In turn, the *tertium non est datur* logic of Rome I and II has no equivalent in the Brussels I Regulation, which internally draws the demarcation line between contractual and non-contractual obligations.

Keywords Brussels I Recast Regulation · Rome I Regulation · Hierarchy · Rule-Exception Relation · Favor Defensoris · Contractual Matters · Party Interests · Tessili Case

3.1 General Scheme

3.1.1 Scaffold of Rome I

Both Regulations consist of a Preamble with Recitals, followed by Articles organised in Chapters which are, as far as the Brussels I Recast Regulation is concerned, further divided into Sections and followed by Annexes. Both Regulations provide for provisions on their relationship with other legal instruments.

The Rome I Regulation deals with contractual obligations and follows the general objective of achieving consistent decisions in conflict of laws cases in different Member States. Within the scope of the Regulation, the courts of all Member States (except Denmark) should apply the same national law. When a claim falls within the scope of the Rome I Regulation, which is described by way of a positive definition and exceptions to it, parties can freely choose the law governing their contract (Article 3). No particular connection between the chosen law and the contractual relationship is required. However, a choice of laws is geographically or substantively limited in a number of cases, most notably to deal with aspects of public policy and to protect the interest of persons considered as the weaker party to a contract. In absence of a party agreement, the governing law will be determined pursuant to the catalogue of conflict rules for eight types of contractual relationships (Article 4), such as contracts for the sales of goods (a), contracts for the provision of services (b), or contracts relating to a right in rem in immovable property (c). If a categorisation fails, the law of the state where the party required to effect the 'characteristic performance' resides will be relevant (para 2). The connecting factors are not rigid, however. If a closer connection to the law of a different state is 'manifest', the law of this State shall be applicable (escape clause[1]). In the event that the contract can neither be subsumed under the catalogue of contracts nor can the characterising feature be determined, the contract will 'be

[1]Article 4(3).

governed by the law of the country with which it is most closely connected' (default rule[2]).

A special regime for contracts of carriage, consumer, insurance, and individual employment is provided by Articles 5–8. The idiosyncrasy of these matters justifies derogations from the general rules. The scope of the applicable law is described by an indicative list comprising, among others, interpretation, performance, or consequences of nullity of the contract (Article 12). Furthermore, the Regulation deals with issues of consent, material and formal validity, and incapacity (Articles 10–13). Burden of proof is governed by Article 18; matters of voluntary assignment, subrogation, multiple debtors, and set-off by Articles 14–17.

Matters of public interest of the forum country and protection of public policy are the concern of rules on 'overriding mandatory provision' and *ordre public*. The priority to the first is given by Article 9(2) (emphasis added): '*Nothing* in this Regulation *shall restrict* the application of the overriding mandatory provisions of the law of the forum'. References are generally understood as references to the domestic law of the respective state, except for the norms on conflict of laws (Article 20, exclusion of *renvoi*).

3.1.2 Scaffold of the Brussels I Recast Regulation

The Brussels I Recast Regulation contains a consistent regime of jurisdiction in civil and commercial matters, which only refers to national law in a few instances. It is accompanied by a system of recognition and enforcement of judgments attaining the free movement of judgements. In line with the Rome I Regulation, the scope of application is described positively and negatively. It also differentiates between provisions applicable to contracts generally and those of specific contracts.

However, its regime is remarkably different from that of the Rome I Regulation as it distinguishes, as a first step, between defendants who are domiciled in a Member State and others who are not. The jurisdiction of each Member State over the latter will, save for some exceptions, be determined by the law of that State. Hence, the personal-territorial scope of Brussels I usually requires the defendant to be domiciled within the EU. A real fallback rule covering almost all claims in civil and commercial matters is established only for defendants who are domiciled in a Member State. They should be sued in the courts of that Member State and only be sued in another Member State by virtue of special rules (Articles 4 and 5). Such defendants can thus expect only to be sued 'at home' unless there is a special rule providing otherwise.

These special jurisdictional rules are exhaustively set out in Sections 2–7 of Chapter II. A list of grounds for 'special jurisdiction' is provided by Article 7, which give credit to the proximity between the contract and the court. Under this

[2]Article 4(4).

provision, additional *fora* are made available to the claimant in certain matters, most importantly in matters relating to a contract (Article 7(1)) and in matters relating to tort, delict or quasi-delict (para 2). Other special jurisdictional rules under Article 7 relate to civil claims for damages or restitution which are based on an act giving rise to criminal proceedings (para 3); a civil claim for the recovery, based on ownership, of a cultural object (para 4); a dispute arising out of the operations of a branch, agency or other establishment (para 5); a dispute brought against a settlor, trustee, or beneficiary of a trust created by the operation of a statute, or by a written instrument, or created orally and evidenced in writing (para 6); and a dispute concerning the payment of remuneration claimed in respect of the salvage of cargo or freight (para 7). The concepts laid down therein must be interpreted independently from national law, taking into account the general scheme and the objectives of the Regulation.[3]

Article 8 concerns joinder and counterclaims, and Article 9 deals with jurisdiction in actions relating to liability from the use or operation of a ship. Articles 10–23 are concerned with protective grounds for jurisdiction: Section 3 sets out jurisdictional rules for matters relating to insurance, Section 4 deals with jurisdiction over consumer contracts, and Section 5 provides for jurisdictional rules over individual contracts of employment. The protective jurisdictional rules limit prorogation of jurisdiction and derogate the general rules of jurisdiction in favour of the weaker party to a contract who may benefit from a *forum actoris*. Article 24 safeguards the exclusive jurisdiction for Member States' courts where there is a particularly strong connection with the dispute, for example, for proceedings which have as their object rights *in rem* in immovable property. Articles 26–26 are concerned with party autonomy: the prorogation of jurisdiction and the submission of the defendant. The Regulation either gives jurisdiction to the courts of a Member State, hence leaving it to the law of that State to specify the local competent court, or directly allocates jurisdiction to a place in a Member State.

In order to avoid conflicting decisions arising from parallel proceedings possible under the Brussels I Recast Regime, and thus to facilitate the administration of justice in the Union,[4] rules on co-ordination are set out in Section 9 of Chapter 2 of the Recast Regulation. These rules must be seen in light of the rules on non-recognition as set out in Chapter III of the Regulation, according to which the recognition of a judgment shall be refused if it is irreconcilable with a judgment given to the same parties in the Member State addressed or with an earlier judgment given in another Member State or in a third State involving the same cause of action and between the same parties (Article 45 litt c-d). A main concern of the Recast Regulation is to prevent risks of non-enforcement as soon as possible, for economic

[3]Case 9/87 *SPRL Arcado v SA Haviland* [1988] ECR 1539 [15]; Case C-189/87, *Athanasios Kalfelis v Bankhaus Schröder* [1988] ECR 5565, [16]; Case 89/91 Shearson Lehmann Hutton Inc.

[4]Report on the Convention on jurisdiction and the enforcement of judgments in civil and commercial matters by Mr P. Jenard [1979] C 59/1, 41.

reasons as well as to guarantee effective access to justice as ensured by Article 6(1) ECHR and European Law.[5] For this purpose, a *lis pendens* rule—*prior tempore, potior jure*—is effective where proceedings involving the same cause of action between the same parties are brought in the courts of different Member States (Article 29). In order to avoid inconsistent decisions, a rule dealing with 'related actions' applies where actions are particularly strongly connected (Article 30). The Brussels I Recast Regulation (1215/2012) updated the Brussels I Regulation (44/2001) and allows Member States' courts to take into account proceedings pending before the courts of third States for the question of whether they stay or continue the proceedings.

The essential aspiration of the European Union to establish a genuine European area of justice in which judicial decisions are able to circulate without restraint is realised by Chapter III: judgments given in a Member State are recognised in all other Member States without the requirement of a special procedure (recognition *ipso iure,* Article 36). A judgment given in a Member State which is enforceable in that Member State shall be enforced under the same conditions as a judgment given in the Member State addressed (Article 41(1)). No declaration of enforceability is required. Article 45 contains a list of reasons for the refusal of recognition (and enforcement) of judgments relating to non-jurisdictional and jurisdictional objections.

An unwritten precondition is formed by the requirement of a cross-border implication; purely internal cases are excluded from its scope. When it comes to the recognition and enforcement of judgments, it is inherent in its system that the Regulation requires the rendition of the judgment by a court situated within the territorial scope of application.

3.2 Hierarchy

3.2.1 The Hierarchy of Brussels I

The presentation of a general rule-special rules relationship under Brussels I should not, however, obscure the true pyramidal hierarchy of the Regulation: the grounds for exclusive jurisdiction (Article 24), which comprise five special rules, are placed on top because they apply regardless of the domicile of the defendant and regardless of any agreement between the parties. For their application, it is sufficient that the subject of litigation is localised in the territory of a Member State. The exclusiveness prevents the application of all other jurisdictional grounds; even deviating jurisdictional agreements cannot overrule it. International jurisdiction is exclusive, whereas the local jurisdiction is to be determined by national law. The justification for the priority of Article 24 is the very close connection between litigation and

[5] Study JLS/C4/2005/03, 174.

Member States.[6] For example, in proceedings which have as their object rights in rem in immovable property or tenancies of immovable property, the courts of the Member State in which the property is situated will have jurisdiction (Article 24 (1)). As this may lead to proceedings in Member States where neither plaintiff nor defendant resides and as parties cannot select another forum, exclusive grounds for jurisdiction must be interpreted in a strict sense.[7] The recognition and enforcement of a judgment may be refused if the court seised unjustifiably exercised jurisdiction under Article 24 (Article 45(e)(ii)).

Prorogation by appearance, privileged jurisdiction over insurance, consumer and employment matters, and prorogation by agreement form the next levels of the hierarchy, all enjoying priority over the general rules, which only formally take the lead in the system of jurisdiction. Where there is an institutional disparity between the parties, the Regulation grants a jurisdictional privilege to insureds, consumers, and employees. Being considered the weaker party to the contract, they are protected by rules of jurisdiction more favourable to their interests than the general rules (Recital 18). Such persons benefit from asymmetric jurisdiction criteria and restrictions of one-sided jurisdiction agreements. A striking innovation has been brought by the reform of the Brussels I Regulation that extended the scope *ratione personarum*, allowing consumers to bring proceedings against the other party to a contract in the courts for the place of his domicile 'regardless of the domicile of the other party' (Article 18(1)). With respect to individual contracts of employment, Article 21 states that an employer not domiciled in a Member State may be sued either in the courts for the place where or from where the employee habitually carries out his work or in the courts for the last place where he did so; or where this is not the case, in the courts for the place where the business which engaged the employee is or was situated.

In terms of autonomy, Brussels I grants a great deal of freedom to the parties to designate their preferred court(s) or to exclude an otherwise competent court. Only cases related to grounds for exclusive jurisdiction and privileged jurisdiction prevail over Article 25. In all other cases, the parties' freedom will be respected. Both choice of forum (Article 25) and jurisdiction by appearance (Article 26) do not require the parties to have their domicile in a Member State. Parties' freedom and the exclusive grounds for jurisdiction already show that there are quite a number of exceptions to the principle that jurisdiction of the courts of each Member State are determined by the law of that Member State if the defendant is not domiciled in a Member State of the European Union. The same holds true for consumer (Article 18(1)) and employee (Article 21(2)) matters.

---

[6]Case C-412/98 *Group Josi Reinsurance Company SA v Universal General Insurance Company* (UGIC) [2000] ECR I-5925; Case C 417/15 *Schmidt v Schmidt* [2016] ECLI:EU:C:2016:881.

[7]Case C-8/98 *Dansommer A/S v Götz* [2000] ECR I-393 [21]; Case 73/77 *Sanders v Van der Putte* [1977] ECR 2383 [17-18]; Case C-115/88 *Reichert and Kockler* [1990] ECR I-27 [9]; Case C-292/93 *Lieber* [1994] ECR I-2535 [12]; C-372/07 *Hasset v The Medical Defence Union* [2008] ECR I-7403 [18]; Case C-605/14 *Komu and others* ECLI:EU:C:2015:833.

The base of the pyramid is formed by the general jurisdictional rule of Article 4, for which the domicile of the defendant—not the subject matter or cause of action—will be decisive. Special grounds of jurisdiction over a defendant domiciled in another Member State (Articles 7–9) allow the claimant to alternatively sue the defendant in the court of a Member State where the defendant has no domicile for the reason of proximity between the action and the court or to facilitate the sound administration of justice.[8] Article 7 sets out a list of additional grounds for jurisdiction, referring to the specific subject-matter of the claim or specific disputes. For example, the special jurisdictional rule for contractual matters (Article 7) reflects the proximity between the contract and the court. It sets out that in matters relating to a contract, a person domiciled in a Member State may also be sued in the courts of the place of performance of the obligation in question. Article 7(2) provides a *forum delicti* rule for matters relating to tort, delict, or quasi-delict: jurisdiction is conferred to the courts for the place where a harmful event occurred or may occur. As a rule, a claim will relate to tort, delict, or quasi-delict when it seeks to establish the liability of the defendant and when it is not related to a contract within the meaning of Article 7(1).[9] Contractual matters under Article 7(1) and matters of tort under Article 7(2) are therefore mutually exclusive.

3.2.2 *The Hierarchy of Rome I*

The hierarchy of Brussels I shows that the jurisdictional[10] rules of the Regulation require a particular link to the forum seised, such as the domicile of the defendant, the location of the subject of litigation, or a prorogation (tacitly[11] or expressly) of forum directing towards a Member State's court. Its system is shaped by a rule-exception relationship.

The Rome I Regulation, too, presents a rule-exception relationship and is guided by a system of proximity-oriented connecting factors. However, its general rules do not generally protect one party to the contract and its formula gives a strong priority to party autonomy. Essentially, the contracting parties have the ability of freely choosing the law governing their contract (Article 3). No connection between the chosen law and the contractual relationship is required. Yet, such a choice has many

[8]Recital 16.

[9]Case C-189/87, *Athanasios Kalfelis v Bankhaus Schröder* [1988] ECR 5565 [18].

[10]It must be noted that the application of the recognition and enforcement provisions does not depend on the domicile of the defendant. Their scope requires the judgment to be rendered by a court or tribunal within the EU. Hence, a judgment given by a national court within the EU against a defendant domiciled outside of the EU can be enforced under the Regulation, even where the jurisdiction is based on national 'exorbitant' grounds for jurisdictions, see Vlas 2007, Article 4, para 76.

[11]Where the defendant enters an appearance under Article 26.

restrictions. First, there are three distinct categories of rules formed to deal with aspects of public policy. The first category relates to 'provisions of the law which cannot be derogated from by agreement'. These provisions are designed to protect mandatory rules in internal cases (Article 3(3)(4)) and in cases where consumer, employee, or rights in *rem* in immovable property are involved. The category of 'overriding mandatory provision' as laid down in Article 9 pursues the goal of protecting matters of public interest of the forum country. Finally, the *ordre public* provision (Article 21) is concerned with the general protection of the public policy of the forum state or that of a third state. There are 'geographical' limitations for passenger contracts (Article 5) and small-risk-insurance contracts (Article 7), where the parties may choose the law of the country only if a territorial relation with the chosen state exists. 'Protective rules' are laid down for specific categories of persons considered as the weaker party to a contract and restrict a choice of law concerning contracts of carriage of passengers (Article 5(2)), consumer contracts (Article 6), insurance contracts (Article 7), and individual employment contracts (Article 8). For example, a choice of law in consumer contracts is valid, but it cannot deprive the consumer of the protection afforded to him by the law applicable by default (principle of favourability).

Where no choice of law has been made, default rules govern the most common types of contractual relationships, which yield to the law of another country than indicated in case of a manifestly closer connection. For example, contracts for the sale of goods and for the provision of services are governed by the law of the country where the seller/service provider has his or her habitual residence. Derogation from the general rules are set out for specific contracts. For example, Article 5(2) lays down a specific rule favouring the law of the country where the passenger has his habitual residence, provided that either the place of departure or the place of destination is situated in that country.

As pointed out earlier, Rome I considers matters of public interest in the form of 'overriding mandatory provisions' (Article 9) and the *ordre public* limitation (Article 21). These options can be used by Member States only in exceptional circumstances. Overriding mandatory provisions are provisions 'the respect for which is regarded as crucial by a country for safeguarding its public interests, such as its political, social or economic organisation, to such an extent that they are applicable to any situation falling within their scope, irrespective of the law otherwise applicable to the contract under this Regulation' (Article 9(1)). They rank on top of the hierarchy as 'nothing in the Rome I Regulation', neither party autonomy nor default rules may restrict its application (Article 9(2)). Article 9(3) allows for application of overriding mandatory provisions of the law of the country of performance of the contractual obligations insofar as those overriding mandatory provisions render the performance of the contract unlawful. The *ordre public* limitation of Article 21 has a similar design. It provides that 'the application of a provision of the law of any country specified by this Regulation may be refused if such application is manifestly incompatible with the public policy of the forum'.

Such situations can only arise where the relevant foreign rule 'departs so radically from the concept of fundamental justice accepted in the forum country that its application would be intolerably offensive to the judicial conscience there.'[12]

3.3 Corresponding Scope and Demarcation Lines

3.3.1 Contractual Matters

The material scope of application is an important factor that must be taken into account to analyse whether there is what is called a 'horizontal consistency',[13] allowing for attribution of identical or similar meaning to identical or similar terms common to both legal acts.

The Brussels I Recast Regulation applies *ratione materiae* to civil and commercial matters regardless of the nature of the court or tribunal before which a matter is brought. It does not apply to 'revenue, customs or administrative matters or to the liability of the State for acts and omissions in the exercise of State authority (*acta iure imperii*) (Article 1(1)).[14] Article 1(2) sets out a catalogue of other 'well-defined matters' (Recital 10), which are exempted from the range of the Regulation's application: issues of legal status, the areas of inheritance, insolvency and social security law, questions of legal capacity, and arbitration procedures. For matters within the material scope of application, Chapter II sets out a system of jurisdictional rules, while Chapter III deals with the recognition and enforcement of judgments.

The Rome I Regulation applies *ratione materiae* to contractual obligations in civil and commercial matters in situations that involve a conflict of laws. Contracts that are formed by organs of a sovereign state in exertion of their authoritative power are outside the scope of application; in particular, the Regulation does not apply to revenue, customs, or administrative matters. The catalogue in Article 1(2) contains a list of contractual situations that are exempted from the ambit of the Regulation. These contractual situations cover, among others, questions involving the status or legal capacity of natural persons, obligations arising out of family relationships or matrimonial property regimes, questions governed by the law of companies and other bodies, and pre-contractual obligations.[15] The *culpa in contrahendo* is governed by Article 12 of the Rome II Regulation providing, as a general rule, that 'the law applicable to a non-contractual obligation arising out of dealings prior to the conclusion of a contract, regardless of whether the contract was

[12]Stone 2010, p. 339.

[13]Crawford and Carruthers 2014, p. 2.

[14]On the term 'civil and commercial matters', see Illmer 2015, p. 61; Case 266/01, *TIARD SA v. Staat der Nederlanden* [2003] ECR I-4867 [28]; Case 814/79, *Netherlands State v. Reinhold Rüffer* [1980] ECR 3807; Case 29/76, *LTU Lufttransportunternehmen GmbH & Co. KG v. Eurocontrol* [1976] ECR 1517.

[15]For an analysis of the excluded matters, see Plender and Wilderspin 2009, pp. 101–129.

actually concluded or not, shall be the law that applies to the contract or that would have been applicable to it had it been entered into'. In other words, the applicable law will be determined by cross-reference to the Rome I Regulation.

Together with the Rome II Regulation, the Rome I and Brussels I Recast Regulations have formed a uniform set of PIL rules for contractual and non-contractual obligations in civil and commercial matters. Since the Rome I Regulation is restricted to contractual obligations, whereas the Brussels I Recast Regulation comprises contractual as well as non-contractual obligations, the corresponding scope is that both Regulations deal with contractual situations in civil and commercial matters while excluding virtually the same matters from their scope of application. The intention to create consistent 'scope and provisions' is expressed by Recital 7 of both Rome I and Rome II Regulations and by the Commission's proposals.[16]

3.3.2 *Demarcation Lines*

Both Regulations have a genuine internal balance and follow different lines of demarcation: Rome I and II cover the entire law of obligations, contractual and non-contractual, and therefore follow a *tertium non est datur* logic,[17] which means that a matter will principally either fall under either one Regulation or the other (save for the matters that are excluded from the scope of application). Falling back into national law for qualification should be avoided. The demarcation between contractual and non-contractual obligations in the Brussels I Recast Regulation follows a different logic: civil and commercial matters that fall neither under the contractual nor non-contractual jurisdiction rules are covered by the general jurisdiction enshrined in Article 4, as long as the defendant is domiciled in a Member State.

That the 'internal economy of each Regulation imposes its own concern on the meaning of definitional terms and these may be at the cost of some broader inconsistencies'[18] can be deduced from ruling in *Falco Privatstiftung*, where the Court held that the concept of service contract under Article 5(1) Brussels Regulation cannot be construed in accordance with the notion of provision of service under Article 50 of the EC Treaty. The point was made that the latter field required, under certain circumstances, a broad interpretation of the concept of services in order to avoid economic activities falling outside the scope of

[16]Proposal for a Regulation of The European Parliament and the Council on the Law Applicable to Non-Contractual Obligations ("Rome II") COM(2003) 427 final; Proposal for a Regulation of the European Parliament and the Council on the law applicable to contractual obligations (Rome I) COM(2005) 650 final.

[17]Freitag 2010, pp. 169–176. For a view on the dividing line between Rome I and Rome II Regulation, see Plender and Wilderspin 2009, p. 47.

[18]Briggs 2014, p. 65, para 2.65.

application of the Treaty. The non-application of the jurisdictional rule for contractual matters under Brussels I, by contrast, does not preclude the contract being subject to other rules governing jurisdiction.[19] By the same token, in *Société Six Constructions/Humbert*, the Court of Justice interpreted Article 5(1) of the Brussels Convention as meaning that 'where the obligation of the employee to carry out the agreed work was performed and had to be performed outside the territory of the Contracting States, Article 5(1) of the Convention is not applicable'. The Court agreed with the Commission that a *forum actoris* should be limited, and consequently, when applying this reason to the criterion of characteristic obligation, it exercised a narrow interpretation of the 'special jurisdiction' since it constitutes 'a derogation from the principle that jurisdiction is vested in the courts of the State of the defendant's domicile'. It is particularly remarkable that the Court acknowledged that there are 'disadvantages in the alternative jurisdiction being precluded by the manner in which the parties to the contract have agreed that it is to be performed' but then referred to the option of the plaintiff to bring an action before the courts of the place of the defendant's domicile, which the Court considered a 'certain and reliable criterion'.[20]

Another example of the genuine internal balance within Brussels I is the ruling *Kainz v Pantherwerke.*[21] The Court of Justice was asked to determine 'the place of the event giving rise to the damage' for the purpose of what is now Article 7(2) of the Brussels I Recast Regulation in cases where a manufacturer faces a claim of liability for a defective product. It is striking that the CJEU, after apodictically referring to the requirement of strict interpretation of special grounds for jurisdiction, localised that place as that at which the product was manufactured by invoking the rationale of the special jurisdiction—that is to say 'a particularly close connecting factor between the dispute and the courts for the place where the harmful event occurred'. At the same time, however, the Court confirmed the 'principle of ubiquity',[22] according to which the place 'where a harmful event occurred or may occur' is either the place where the harmful event giving rise to the damage occurred or the place where the actual damage occurred, with the notable result that the claimant may sue the defendant in the courts of either of those places.[23] Even more striking, the Court carried out this reasoning without defining the place of manufacture and without explaining wherein the particularly close link was established. Most striking is that the Court rejected the possibility to obtain

---

[19]Case C-533/07 *Falco Privatstiftung v Weller-Lindhorst* [2009] ECR I-3327 [34-38]; see also Opinion of Advocate General Trstenjak delivered on 27 January 2009 to Case C-533/07, para 73: 'It must be considered that the legal concepts relevant to a particular branch of law are always stated strictly in relation to the field involved, so that a definition valid for one sector cannot be transposed directly to another'.

[20]Case 32/88 *Société Six Constructions/Humbert* [1989] ECR I-341 [20].

[21]Case C-45/13 EU:C:2014:7; discussed in ecolex 2014, p. 334 (Schmon).

[22]Paragraph 23.

[23]Paragraph 27.

guidance for the determination of the liability claim from the Directive 85/374/EEC concerning liability for defective products or the Rome II Regulation, which contains specific conflict rules on product liability that focus on the place where the product was ‘marketed’.

3.4 Rule Exception Relationship in Favour of the Defendant

3.4.1 Actor Sequitur Forum Rei

The Rome I Regulation determines the law considered the most suitable one to govern a contractual situation and provides for escape clauses guaranteeing the application of the law of another State where a closer connection to that law is manifest. It therefore follows the traditional ideal-theoretical conflict-of-laws-doctrine, according to which only a single *lex cause* shall be applicable. It rejects a general favourability principle as this undermines foreseeability and unduly benefits one party to the contract. This shows an elementary difference to the approach of the Brussels I Recast Regulation, which prefers a rule-exception relation in favour of the defendant. In view of the fact that it is even more difficult to ‘defend oneself in the courts of a foreign country than in those of another town in the country where one is domiciled’,[24] *actor sequitur forum rei*—not the closest or best place of jurisdiction—was chosen as the guiding maxim of the Brussels I Recast Regulation.[25] The often overstated argument is that the claimant must bear the burden of seeking the place of the defendant because he would be the aggressor who disturbs the *status quo*.[26] Rules on special jurisdiction take the subject-matter in dispute into account and, at the same time, compensate claimants in that they can make use of additional *fora*. ‘The reason for that rule, which reflects an objective of proximity, is the existence of a close link between the contract and the court called upon to hear and determine the case.’[27] It complies with continental European traditions of litigation that the defendant’s *forum domicilii* shall, save for some exceptions, always be available.

---

[24]Report on the Convention on jurisdiction and the enforcement of judgments in civil and commercial matters by Mr P. Jenard [1979] C 59/1, 18.

[25]Certainly, the defendant might, in individual cases, prefer a forum that is not located in the State of his domicile. Article 4 of the Recast Regulation therefore protects the *typical* interest of the defendant. For general comments on this principle, see Pfeiffer 1995, pp. 599–603.

[26]Von Mehren 2002, p. 181; Schack 2002, p. 89. For an overview of viewpoints, see Buchner 1998, pp. 16–18.

[27]Case C-386/05, *Color Drack GmbH v Lexx International Vertriebs GmbH* [2007] I-03,699 [22]; Case C-204/08 *Rehder* ECR [2009] I-6073.

3.4.2 *Strict Interpretation of Special Grounds for Jurisdiction*

Certainly, the availability of a forum at the domicile of the defendant as such would not realise a *favor defensoris* model, which demands, in addition, a restrictive interpretation of special grounds for jurisdiction over a defendant domiciled in another Member State. The existence of a rule-exception relationship in favour of the defendant cannot be deduced simply from the system of the Brussels Convention/(Recast) Regulation since general jurisdiction by virtue of Article 4 could simply be understood as a rule which serves the interest of the claimant as always having a legal venue available.[28] In addition, the availability of this forum has the advantage that the claimant can immediately enforce the judgment.[29] The term ‘special jurisdiction’ is not significant in this respect either. Grounds for special jurisdiction are special in that they require a relationship to the subject-matter of the claim, whereas the ‘general’ jurisdiction serves as a safe haven for all claims in civil and commercial matters.

However, the intention to protect the defendant (more than the claimant) becomes evident in the Report of Jenard and likewise in the clarification of Article 5 of the Brussels I Recast Regulation, stating that only grounds for special jurisdiction enable the claimant to bring a proceeding before the court of *another* Member State. In the judgment *Falco Privatstiftung*, mentioned earlier, the Court not only explained the internal economy of the Regulation but also confirmed the long-standing case law that the broad logic and scheme of the rules governing jurisdiction require a narrow interpretation of the rules on special jurisdiction, which derogate from the general principle that jurisdiction is based on the defendant’s domicile. An illustrative example is the case *Kalfelis v Schröder*, where the Court held to the special jurisdiction provided for in Article 6 of the Brussels Convention that there must be a connection between the claims made against each of the defendants. Otherwise, the plaintiff must be denied ‘the liberty to make a claim against a number of defendants with the sole object of ousting the jurisdiction of the courts of the State where one of the defendants is domiciled’.[30] Already a few years earlier, the Court stressed the interplay of the jurisdictional rules with those on the recognition and enforcement of judgments and held that the protection of the rights of the defendant ‘serves as a counterpoise’ to the facilities as regards the free movement of judgments.[31]

---

[28]Buchner 1998, p. 5.

[29]See opinion of General Advocate Ruiz-Jarabo Colomer, 14 March 2006, Case C-103/05 *Reisch Montage AG v Kiesel Baumaschinen Handels GmbH* [2006] ECR I-06,827, para 21; see also Pfeiffer 1995, p. 502.

[30]Case C-189/87 *Athanasios Kalfelis v Bankhaus Schröder* [1988] ECR 5565 [8-9].

[31]Case C-220/84 *AS-Autoteile Service GmbH v Malhé* [1985] ECR I-2267 [15].

3.4.3 *Avoidance of Forum Actoris*

The intention of Brussels I is thus to restrict a *forum actoris* to particular situations for a derogation of the justice model of Union law on jurisdiction should be avoided.[32] That the negation or ignorance of this rationale on the level of interpretation may have unsatisfying jurisdictional consequences was demonstrated by the *Tessili* ruling. The Court of Justice held that, for the purposes of Article 5(1) Brussels Convention (which is now Article 7(1)a), 'the place of performance' ought to be determined by the *lex causae* because 'it does not appear possible to give any more substantial guide to its interpretation', due to the current lack of unification in the national substantive laws.[33] The ruling raised harsh critiques[34] for a couple of reasons: For example, it was considered that the assessment of jurisdiction by the courts 'shall not be burdened and hampered with incidental questions of substantive law if possible'.[35] The (indirect) reference to the applicable law to determine jurisdiction was also rejected for the reason that it ignored procedural justice:[36] in cases of claims concerning pecuniary obligations, the claimant could be granted a home-match even where the designated court has no close connection with the facts of the case. An influential opinion was delivered by GA Lenz[37] to *Custom Made Commercial v Stawa Metallbau* where he attacked the view of the Court that the debtor should be answerable in the court for the place where he had to perform his obligation under the rules of the substantive law. The GA mindfully explained the purpose of determining the place of performance of obligations to make payment under the substantive law and concluded that 'the purely economic allocation of risks' has nothing to do with the 'question whether the debtor has to accept the creditor's suing him at a particular place'.

This critique ultimately culminated in the reduction of the impact of the *Tessili*-doctrine by introducing an autonomous definition 'of the place of performance of the obligation in question' for the important cases of the sale of goods and the provision of services into Article 5(1)(b) of the Brussels I Regulation, which is now Article 7(1)(b). For tort claims, the *Brogsitter*[38] decision of the Court made clear that civil liability claims may be considered matters relating to a contract under the

[32]For the justice model of the United States, see Buchner 1998, pp. 24–42.

[33]Case C-12/76 *Tessili v Dunlop AG* [1976] ECR 1473 [14].

[34]See Mankowski 2007, p. 200 (and references there); Pfeiffer 1995, p. 679 (law on jurisdiction serves particular procedural purposes, which demand an autonomous interpretation of legal terms). See, however, Geimer 1983, § 83 II 2 (arguing that the debtor should answer before the courts of the state where he fulfils his obligations).

[35]Mankowski 2007, p. 160.

[36]Basedow 2001, p. 593; Pfeiffer 1995, pp. 677–679.

[37]See also the supporting opinions of Advocate General Ruiz-Jarabo Colomer (C-440/97) and Advocate General Léger (C-420/97).

[38]Case C-548/12, *Marc Brogsitter v Fabrication de Montres Normandes EURL, Karsten Fräßdorf*, ECLI:EU:C:2014:148.

Regulation even though they would qualify as tort claims under the national law of obligations. In *Granarolo*, the Court specified that it is up to the national court to determine the nature of the claim at the outset of the proceedings, taking into account the specific circumstances of the case which has been brought forward before it.[39]

3.5 Weighing of Party Interests and Antinomies

3.5.1 *Congruence with Rome I at Stake?*

The scheme of the Rome I Regulation broadly follows the principle of proximity and closest connection. It focuses on the residence of the characteristic performer and consequently benefits the seller, who sees his home law applied. The general rules of party autonomy and default rules are accompanied by a special regime for particular contracts: Contracts of carriage, for consumer contracts, for insurance contracts, and individual employment contracts derogate from the general rules as they restrict party autonomy and follow a different way of selecting the applicable law where no choice of law has been made. The Brussels I Regulation follows proximity considerations as well, however, it seeks to balance the protection of the defendant with the availability of fact-oriented places for jurisdiction. It can therefore be concluded that the subordination to the *favor defensoris* will have an influence on the qualification of certain matters.

3.5.2 *Broad Interpretation of Contractual Matters*

Nevertheless, the requirement to strictly interpret the special grounds for jurisdiction does not necessarily require a strict interpretation of the notion of 'matters relating to contract'. On the contrary, the rulings by the Court of Justice according to which neither a reciprocal relationship between the contractual parties nor a conclusion of a contract is required, demonstrate that the contractual concept under Article 7 is understood in a broad sense. It is not to be interpreted narrowly.[40] The respective contractual provisions have a common core that consists of an (alleged) obligation freely assumed by one person against another person. This view was confirmed in *ERGO Insurance v If P&C Insurance & Gjensidige Baltic v PZU*

[39]Case C-196/15, *Granarolo SpA v Ambrosi Emmi France SA* [2016] ECLI:EU:C:2016:559 [25].

[40]For example, C-27/02, *Engler v Janus Versand GmbH*, 2005 I-481, ECLI:EU:C:2005:33 [48] ('it follows from the foregoing that, as the Advocate General pointed out in point 38 of his Opinion, the concept of 'matters relating to contract' referred to in Article 5(1) of the Brussels Convention is not interpreted narrowly by the Court').

Lietuva.[41] Where an action falls under special jurisdiction for contractual matters under Article 7(1) of the Brussels I Recast Regulation, the Rome I Regulation will likely also be applicable. Certainly, regard must be given to the matters exempted from its scope.[42]

Hence, the formal reference in case-law to the rule-exception relationship between general and special jurisdictional grounds is one thing, the classification in concrete cases quite another. A blind rule-exception mechanism should be rejected anyway. The mere fact that a provision is an exception to the general rule might[43] prohibit an extensive interpretation—*singularia non sunt extendenda*—because the exception shall not become the rule. Yet, what is not justified is an interpretation that undermines the *ratio legis* of the provision in question. Any legislative provision, general rule or exception, has a proper meaning which must be determined in light of the purpose, wording, scheme, and object of the legal instrument to which it belongs.[44] For the same reasons, exceptions are even open to analogies because they contain a *ratio legis* which can principally be used to give meaning to another rule that follows the same rationale.[45] It is therefore critical to identify the rationale by using evaluative reasoning.

3.5.3 Strict Interpretation of Special Protective Provisions?

Evaluative arguments can also be used to reject the application of a particularly strict exception-relation in favour of the defendant when it comes to the categories of market participants which are considered ‘weak’: employees, passengers, insurance policyholders, and consumers alike. Under the Regulations, these persons are protected by rules that are more favourable to their interests than the general rules.[46] In contrast to the subject-related grounds for jurisdictions, two types of personal-related jurisdiction are on trial—not party interests versus subject matter—and the scale is tipped towards the protection of the weaker party to the contract, may he be claimant or defendant. The objective to protect the defendant as the party to a litigation who is considered as generally having the weaker position is trumped by the objective of protecting the party who is considered as generally having the

---

[41]Joint Cases C 359/14 and C 475/14 [2016] ECLI:EU:C:2016:40 [44] (‘By analogy, and in accordance with the aim of consistency’ [...]).

[42]Opinion of Advocate General Kokott, delivered on 31 January 2019 to Case C-25/18, ECLI:EU:C:2019:86 [60] (referring to questions governed by the law of companies).

[43]Schwartze 2015, p. 66 (exceptions not necessarily to be interpreted strictly); Kramer 2010, p. 206 (arguing that a legislative focus on a rule-exception relation does not in the least mean that the *lex singularis* will continue to be an exception in the practical application of law, e.g., the exception could ‘eat up the rule’; evaluative arguments must be the focus).

[44]See opinion of GA Jacaobs, 13 December 2001 to C-96/00 *Gabriel* [2002] ECR I-6367, 46.

[45]Bydlinski 1991, p. 440; Larenz 1991, p. 355.

[46]Recital 23 of Rome I; Recital 18 of Brussels I.

weaker position in a contractual relationship. There are thus good reasons to not invoke the *favor defensoris* argument to justify a particularly strict interpretation of the protective grounds for jurisdiction; at least insofar as the imbalance of the parties is clear.

A strict interpretation would also amplify antinomies in relation to the Rome I Regulation, which does not follow a *favor defensoris* principle. It could result in a lack of congruence of forum and law in consumer contract cases. So far, the Court of Justice did not pay much attention to this problem. It has put emphasis on the rule-exception rationale of the Brussels system of jurisdiction and justified a particularly restrictive approach with the argument that the consumer protective provisions derogate twofold: from the jurisdictional ground for contracts and from the general grounds for jurisdiction. On the other hand, recent case law is rather permissive and general jurisprudence is devised by an attempt to reconcile the need for protection of the weaker party with the commitment to avoid an extension of the scope of Article 17(c) of the Recast Regulation. This will be discussed in Chap. 8.

3.5.4 Court Accepts Classification Problems

Also, case law shows that the Court, on some occasions, seems to be willing to accept classification problems for the sake of harmony. A preventive action brought by a consumer protection organisation for the purpose of preventing a trader from using unfair terms in contracts with private individuals is a matter relating to tort, delict, or quasi-delict within the meaning of Article 7(2) of the Recast Regulation.[47] As regards the applicable law, the Court of Justice explicitly referred *in Verein für Konsumenteninformation v Amazon*[48] to the aim of consistent application of the Brussels I, Rome I, and Rome II (Recitals 7) Regulations and considered an action for injunction as relating to a non-contractual obligation arising out of a tort/delict within the meaning of the Rome II Regulation. On the other hand, the law applicable to the examination of the unfairness of terms in consumer contracts which are the subject of the injunction must be determined independently in accordance with the nature of those terms, hence in accordance with the Rome I Regulation. This approach is astonishing because of the absence between any contractual relationship between the consumer protection organisation and the defendant professional. Indeed, there are good arguments that the classification of a contractual obligation under conflict of laws should not depend on the identity of the parties. However, an injunctive action is abstract; at its core there is no actual obligation freely assumed

[47]Case C-167/00 *Verein für Konsumenteninformation v Henkel* [2002] I-8111.

[48]Case C-191/15 [2016] ECLI:EU:C:2016:612.

by one party against another. It is not brought in the place of the consumer[49] by way of assignment or subrogation, but rather the protection of the collective interest of consumers is at stake. The distinction by the Court therefore effects a somewhat artificial consistency of individual and representative actions, paying attention to a 'uniform application'[50] of Rome I and Rome II. It does not consider whether Rome I may be more suitable only to individual questions and seems to disregard the implications in terms of access to justice for consumers.[51]

3.6 Conclusions

Each Regulation has its own internal economy and specific demarcation lines. Brussels I is driven by the thought of providing access to the courts of the EU Member State where the defendant is domiciled. For procedural justice reasons, this party should be better protected than the claimant, who, in turn, can make use of additional fora if the subject-matter of the dispute allows it. Rome I cannot be concerned with such jurisdictional thoughts. Its rules do not generally protect one party to the contract and its formula gives a strong priority to party autonomy. There is thus no parallel feature to 'general jurisdiction' in conflict of laws, as a default rule would thwart its idea of qualification. In turn, the 'tertium non est datur' logic of Rome I and II has no equivalent in the Brussels I Regulation, which internally draws the demarcation line between contractual and non-contractual obligations.

What unites both legal acts is that they keep in mind the idea of proximity to the dispute or legal relationship and feature a rule-exception relationship between general and special rules.

References

Basedow J (2001) Die Auslegung von EG-Verordnungen. In: Basedow J et al. (eds) Aufbruch nach Europa: 75 Jahre Max-Planck-Institut für Privatrecht. Mohr Siebeck, Tübingen, pp 583–594

Briggs A (2014) Private International Law in English Courts. Oxford University Press, Oxford

Buchner B (1998) Kläger- und Beklagtenschutz im Recht der internationalen Zuständigkeit: Lösungsansätze für eine zukünftige Gerichtsstands- und Vollstreckungskonvention. Mohr Siebeck, Tübingen

Bydlinski F (1991) Methodenlehre. Springer, Vienna

---

[49]Opinion of Advocate General Saugmandsgaard delivered on 2 June 2016 to Case C-191/15, para 54.

[50]Case C-191/15, n.48 [53].

[51]For a dogmatic discussion, see Micklitz and Reich (2015) p. 181.

Crawford EB, Carruthers JM (2014) Connection and Coherence between and among European Instruments in the Private International Law of Obligations. ICLQ 64:1–29

Freitag R (2010) Rom I, Rom II – tertium est datur im Kollisionsrecht der Schuldverhältnisse – Anmerkungen zum sachlichen Anwendungsbereich der Verordnungen Rom I und Rom I. In: Bernreuther J et al (eds) Festschrift für Ulrich Spellenberg zum 70. Geburtstag. Sellier, Munich, pp 169–176

Geimer R (1983) Band I/1. In: Geimer R, Schütze RA (eds) Internationale Urteilsanerkennung. Beck, Munich, § 83 II 2

Illmer M (2015) Scope and Definitions. In: Dickinson A, Lein E (eds) The Brussels I Regulation Recast. Oxford University Press, New York, pp 55–92

Kramer EA (2010) Juristische Methodenlehre. Beck, Munich

Larenz K (1991) Methodenlehre der Rechtswissenschaft. Springer, Berlin

Mankowski P (2007) Art 5. In: Magnus U, Mankowski P (eds) Brussels I Regulation: European Commentaries on Private International Law. Sellier, European Law Publishers, Germany, pp 77–236

Micklitz H, Reich N (2015) Das IPR der Verbraucherverbandsklage gegen missbräuchliche AGB. EWS 4:181–193

Pfeiffer T (1995) Internationale Zuständigkeit und prozessuale Gerechtigkeit: Die internationale Zuständigkeit im Zivilprozess zwischen effektivem Rechtsschutz und nationaler Zuständigkeitspolitik. Klostermann, Frankfurt/Main

Plender R, Wilderspin M (2009) The European Private International Law of Obligations, 3rd edn. Sweet & Maxwell, London

Schack H (2002) Internationales Zivilverfahrensrecht, 3rd edn. Beck, Munich

Schwartze A (2015) Die Rechtsvergleichung. In: Riesenhuber K (ed) Europäische Methodenlehre: Handbuch für Ausbildung und Praxis, 3rd edn. Beck, Berlin, pp 53–69

Stone P (2010) EU Private International Law, 2nd edn. Elgar European Law, Cheltenham

Vlas P (2007) Arts 2-4. In: Magnus U, Mankowski P (eds) Brussels I Regulation: European Commentaries on Private International Law. Sellier European Law Publishers, Munich, pp 69–77

Von Mehren AT (2002) Theory and Practice of Adjudicatory Authority in Private International Law: General Course of Private International Law. 295 Recueil Des Cours, pp 9–34

Chapter 4
Selected Concepts

Contents

Abstract The genetic affinity and complementarity of the Brussels I Recast and Rome I Regulation suggest a systematic approach when interpreting legal terms common to both legal acts. There are many commonalities between the Regulations, such as the notion of civil and commercial matters or the important concepts of 'direct activity' or 'sale of goods'. The contractual concept has a common core, which consists of a legal obligation freely assumed by one person against another. In most of the cases, a contract can thus always be called a contract. Differences remain, nevertheless. Application criteria do not entirely correspond and do not follow the same delimitation lines and the connecting factors are shaped by the underlying rationale of conflict of laws and procedural law respectively. For

C. Schmon, *The Interconnection of the EU Regulations Brussels I Recast and Rome I*, Short Studies in Private International Law,
https://doi.org/10.1007/978-94-6265-367-2_4

example, the concept of habitual residence is of limited relevance in the Brussels I Recast Regulation, whilst it is, typical of a conflict of laws legal act, the main connecting factor throughout the Rome I Regulation.

Keywords Civil and Commercial Matters · Concept of Domicile · Concept of Habitual Residence · Contractual Matters · Sale of Goods · Provision of Services · Ilsinger Case · Direct Activity · Place of Performance · Alpenhof Case

4.1 Civil and Commercial Matters

The Brussels I Recast and the Rome Regulations lack a positive definition of what constitutes 'civil and commercial matters' wherefore much academic literature is dedicated to the delimitation of this concept. For the purpose of this chapter, it will be sufficient to briefly outline what 'civil and commercial matters' entails whilst referring to academic doctrine for an in-depth analysis. It is widely accepted that the term 'civil and commercial matters' should be understood as bearing the same meaning in both Regulations and that an autonomous interpretation is required to ensure uniformity in all Member States. With respect to the Brussels I Recast Regulation, a detachment of the European legal act from national conceptions is already implied by Article 1, which explains that it applies *ratione materiae* to civil and commercial matters *regardless* of the nature of the court or tribunal before which a matter is brought. An autonomous understanding also follows from case law. The Court of Justice has emphasised the independent concept of 'civil and commercial matters' many times, stressing that an interpretation should primarily be carried out by reference to the objectives and scheme of the Brussels I Regulation (Convention) and only secondarily by reference to general principles stemming from national legal systems.[1] In earlier judgments, the Court focused on whether the claim would be regarded as private or public across the Member States. Over time, it has adjusted its approach towards a methodology which focuses on the legal right asserted. What is required is an assessment of whether the legal right is one which forms part of the ordinary civil law of that state or whether it is part of its public law.[2] Thus, a claim may fall in the material scope even if it is asserted by or against public authorities.

[1]C-292/05 *Irini Lechouritou and Others v Dimosio tis Omospondiakis Dimokratias tis Germanias* [2007] ECR I-1519 [29]; Case C-29/76 *LTU* [1976] ECR 1541 [3, 5]; Case C-814/79 *Rüffer* [1980] ECR 3807 [7]; Case C-271/00 *Baten* [2002] ECR I-10489 [28]; Case C-266/01 *Préservatrice foncière TIARD* [2003] ECR I-4867 [20].

[2]Briggs (2014), pp. 189–192.

4.2 Domicile and Habitual Residence

4.2.1 Multiple Criteria Under the Brussels I Recast Regulation

Typical for a civil procedural law act, the Brussels I Recast gives significant authority to the concept of 'domicile' for the purpose of determining jurisdiction. It shapes, for example, the grounds for general jurisdiction, and whether or not the defendant is domiciled in a Member State will influence the applicability of the jurisdictional rules of the Regulation. However, a uniform definition is provided only for corporations and associations while reference is made to the law of each Member State to determine whether an individual, natural person is domiciled in that State.[3] For corporations and associations, the Regulation sets out three criteria: a company or other legal person or association of natural or legal persons is domiciled at the place where it has its (a) statutory seat, (b) central administration, or (c) principal place of business (Article 63).[4] It follows that under the Brussels I Recast Regulation, a person may have several domiciles.

While the concept of 'habitual residence' is of limited relevance in the Brussels I Recast Regulation, it is—typical of a conflict of laws legal act—the main connecting factor throughout the Rome I Regulation to determine the law applicable to contractual obligations. The Court of Justice will thus likely refer to the Brussels II *bis* Regulation[5] or other EU instruments[6] to give meaning to it.

[3]Article 62(1): In order to determine whether a party is domiciled in the Member State whose courts are seised of a matter, the court shall apply its internal law. (2) If a party is not domiciled in the Member State whose courts are seised of the matter, then, in order to determine whether the party is domiciled in another Member State, the court shall apply the law of that Member State.

[4]Article 63(2) provides that, 'for the purposes of Ireland, Cyprus and the United Kingdom, 'statutory seat' means the registered office or, where there is no such office anywhere, the place of incorporation or, where there is no such place anywhere, the place under the law of which the formation took place. 3. In order to determine whether a trust is domiciled in the Member State whose courts are seised of the matter, the court shall apply its rules of private international law.'

[5]Council Regulation (EC) No 2201/2003 of 27 November 2003 concerning jurisdiction and the recognition and enforcement of judgments in matrimonial matters and the matters of parental responsibility, repealing Regulation (EC) No 1347/2000 [2003] OJ L 388/1. The Regulation is oriented to the work of the Hague Conference; the Hague Conventions regularly use the concept of 'habitual residence'.

[6]Council Regulation (EC) No 4/2009 of 18 December 2008 on jurisdiction, applicable law, recognition and enforcement of decisions and cooperation in matters relating to maintenance obligations [2009] L 7/1 (Maintenance Regulation); Regulation (EU) 650/2012 of the European Parliament and of the Council of 4 July 2012 on jurisdiction, applicable law, recognition and enforcement of decisions and acceptance and enforcement of authentic instruments in matters of succession and on the creation of a European Certificate of Succession [2012] L 201/107 (Succession Regulation); Council Regulation (EU) No 1259/2010 of 20 December 2010 implementing enhanced cooperation in the area of the law applicable to divorce and legal separation [2010] L 343/10 (Divorce Regulation).

It is asserted that the flexibility of the connecting factor 'habitual residence' lies in the fact that factual elements, such as time, whereabouts, and working place, are taken into account. Even intentions may be relevant. The Brussels II *bis* Regulation, for example, employed the concept of habitual residence because it could be better applied to 'matters affecting persons in a time of personal crisis, where they often move from one country to another'. On the other hand, it is usually easier to determine the 'domicile' of a person, especially in typical civil law jurisdictions that provide for a register of domicile.[7] Indeed, it is easy to think about a case in which a person is registered in one country but habitually resides in another. It is also true that the orientation towards factual elements fits perfectly with the conflict of laws rationale of the 'closest connection' to the facts. In contrast, except for the area of family where the assessment of close ties is crucial, law of jurisdiction struggles with instable connecting factors and strives for clear concepts.

However, neither the term 'habitual residence' nor 'domicile' are concepts of facts.[8] They are terms of art, which need to be concretised and interpreted by judges and which may or may not employ clarity and legal certainty or provide for flexibility and equity. As far as the Brussels I Recast Regulation is concerned, the Jenard Report reveals that the concept of 'habitual residence' was rejected because 'the term "habitual" was open to conflicting interpretations, since the laws of some of the Member States provide that an entry in the population registers is conclusive proof of habitual residence.'[9] 'Domicile' was not chosen as the main point of reference because it serves as a stabile connecting factor but for the reason that the majority of the Member States used it as a basis of jurisdiction. For its concretisation, the Regulation does not opt for an autonomous approach but, instead, sets out a complex multiple referral to the *lex fori* of the court seised to determine whether a party is domiciled in that Member State and, in order to determine whether the party is domiciled in another Member State, to the law of that country (Article 62). For determination of the domicile of a legal person (Article 63), multiple criteria are provided. Concerning trusts, however, a domestic law approach is relevant. From all this follows that whether the term 'domicile' is employed in fact clarity or legal certainty will essentially depend on whether there is a uniform definition and whether the concept is defined in a narrow way.

---

[7]Kruger 2008, p. 73.

[8]For the conclusion that the term 'habitual residence' is a 'concept of fact', see Baetge 1994, pp. 105–106.

[9]Report on the Convention on jurisdiction and the enforcement of judgments in civil and commercial matters by Mr. P. Jenard [1979] C 59/1, 15.

4.2.2 Single Criterion Under Rome I

Recital 39 of the Rome I Regulation gives a remarkable legislative response to the broad concept of 'domicile' for non-natural persons under Brussels I. It rejects such an approach for its lack of legal certainty and explains that Rome I, instead, follows a clear definition of habitual residence to enable parties to foresee the law applicable to their situation.

Accordingly, Article 19 states that the habitual residence of companies and other bodies, corporate or unincorporated, is the place of central administration. The principal place of business will be relevant for determining the residence of natural persons who act in the course of their business activity. Rome I thus consciously refers to a single criterion to establish the habitual residence of companies and other bodies in order to avoid the problems which may arise from the normative concept of 'domicile' of legal entities under the Brussels I Recast Regulation which, notably, provides for additional determinations for the 'statutory seat' for Ireland, Cyprus and the United Kingdom.[10] Ironically, Recital 15 of the Brussels I Recast Regulation explains that the purpose of the autonomous definition is to 'make the common rules more transparent and avoid conflicts of jurisdiction'. However, as regards the domicile of natural persons who act outside of their business activity, Rome I fails to provide an autonomous definition.

4.3 The Contract

4.3.1 Contractual Obligations Versus Contractual Matters

While the uniform understanding of the concept of 'civil and commercial matters' is beyond dispute, the determination of 'contract' is more difficult. Rome I speaks of 'contractual obligations', whereas its procedural counterpart uses the term 'matters relating to a contract' in Articles 7(1)(a) and 17. The different phrasing makes it challenging to comprehend the scope of application and to define a clear line of demarcation between contractual and non-contractual obligations. Since national courts should have the power to examine whether they have jurisdiction in order to ensure the legal effect of the special jurisdiction in matters relating to a contract, the Court of Justice ruled that Article 5(1) of the Brussels Regulation (which is now Article 7(1)) comprises matters where the existence of a contract is in question or where a party has failed to comply with a contractual obligation.[11] This corresponds

[10]Paragraph 2 states that, "for the purposes of Ireland, Cyprus and the United Kingdom, 'statutory seat' means the registered office or, where there is no such office anywhere, the place of incorporation or, where there is no such place anywhere, the place under the law of which the formation took place".

[11]Case 38/81 *Effer SpA v Hans-Joachim Kantner* [1981] ECR 825 [7].

to Article 10 of the Rome I Regulation providing that both existence and validity of a contract will be determined by the law which would govern it under the Regulation if the contract were valid. On the other hand, the concept of 'contractual obligation' implies the actual existence of an obligation, hence exempting pre-contractual obligations (*culpa in contrahendo*) from the ambit of the Regulation (as clarified by Article 1(2)), notwithstanding 'whether the contract was actually concluded or not'. This definition cannot be found in the Rome I Regulation but is provided in Article 12 of the Rome II Regulation, which, however, submits such claims to the *lex contractus in negotio*.

4.3.2 A Freely Assumed Obligation

The Court of Justice held on various occasions that the phrase 'matters relating to a contract' must be interpreted independently and the concept of Article 5(1) (now Article 7) (only) requires the existence of an obligation freely assumed by one party against another.[12] Accordingly, a direct action of a sub-purchaser of goods against the manufacturer, who is not the seller, for defects in those goods will not fall under the special jurisdiction. By implication, neither of the Regulations seem to require a *do ut des*-relationship. That the respective contractual provisions have a common core that consists of an (alleged) obligation freely assumed by one person against another person was confirmed in *ERGO Insurance*.[13] The Court of Justice expressly referred to the case law on the Brussels I Regulation and considered, by analogy and in light of the objective to ensure consistency, that the concept of contractual obligation within the meaning of Article 1 of the Rome I Regulation designates a legal obligation freely consented to by one person towards another.

From this follows that where an action falls under special jurisdiction for contractual matters under Article 7(1) of the Brussels I Recast Regulation, the Rome I Regulation will likely also be applicable. Certainly, regard must be given to the matters exempted from its scope.[14] However, a differentiation is made as to the parties to the contract. For consumer contracts, contracts must be *concluded* between the parties. The case law on 'prize notifications'—letters that are sent from businesses to consumers creating the impression that a prize would be awarded to them in order to induce them to place an order—is illustrative for this

[12]C-34/82 *Peteres v ZNAV* [1983] ECR 987; C-26/91, *Jakob Handte v TMCS* [1992] ECR I-3967; C-334/00 *Tacconi v HWS* [2002] ECR I-7357 [23]. See also Case C-196/15, *Granarolo SpA v Ambrosi Emmi France SA* [2016] ECLI:EU:C:2016:559 [25-26] where the Court gave criteria to establish whether an action for damages founded on an abrupt termination of a long-standing business relationship may be considered as contractual.

[13]Joint Cases C-359/14 and C-475/14 [2016] ECLI:EU:C:2016:40 [44] ('By analogy, and in accordance with the aim of consistency' [...]).

[14]Opinion of Advocate General Kokott, delivered on 31 January 2019 to Case C-25/18, ECLI:EU:C:2019:86 [60] (referring to questions governed by the law of companies).

systematisation and the development of the concept of consumer contracts in private international law. Austrian and German laws aim to punish such a business tactic by allowing the consumer to bring proceedings before a court to enforce the price that was promised, even in cases where no order was placed and where recipients never expected to get any reward.[15] Therefore, the question arose of how to classify obligations that lack a *do ut des* relationship. In *Ilsinger*,[16] the Court held that such claims are covered by Article 15(1)(c) of the Brussels I Regulation, 'on condition that the professional vendor has undertaken in law to pay that prize to the consumer [or], where that condition has not been fulfilled, such proceedings are covered [by the Regulation] only if the consumer has in fact placed an order with that professional vendor.' The Court explained that it is necessary for the business 'to assume such a legal obligation by submitting a firm offer which is sufficiently clear and precise with regard to its object and scope as to give rise to a link of a contractual nature as referred to by that provision'.[17] No reciprocal obligations were required, but a contract must have been *concluded* between a business and a consumer. If this was not the case, the contract would 'at most be liable to be classified as pre-contractual or quasi contractual and might therefore, where appropriate, be covered solely by Article 5(1) of that regulation'.[18] It remains to be seen whether Article 6 of the Rome I Regulation will cover prize notifications that fall under Article 17 of the Brussels I Recast Regulation.

4.3.3 *Tort and Delict and Third-Party Obligations*

The criteria set out in Articles 7(1) and 7(2) do not entirely correspond to the criteria that describe the material scope of application of the Rome Regulations. Article 7 (2) refers to 'matters relating to tort, delict or quasi-delict'. It establishes jurisdiction for the liability of the defendant for damages. It follows that Article 7(2) will not cover claims for restitution of unjust enrichment or vindication of property, arguably not relating to liability for damage. Claims for the reversal of unjust enrichment are dealt with by the Rome II Regulation. Where, however, the enrichment arises in connection with a supposed contract, the *lex contractus* will probably

[15]Although Austrian law refers to the 'reasonable consumer', who is generally interested in receiving and processing information and generally smart enough to consider these information before making a decision, the requirements are rather low: the leeway within which the entrepreneur has to pay apparently ends only at notifications, leaving no doubt that the 'winner' is to be determined otherwise. Average attention and simple efforts to capture the information of the entrepreneur are sufficient to take the promise in the letter literally; see OGH 1 Ob 303/02v (Austrian Supreme Court) [2003] EvBl 2003, 464. The reason for such an imminent limitation of contractual freedom is the idea of substantial fairness and, on the other hand, considerations rooted in competition law.

[16]Case C-180/06 *Ilsinger v Dreschers* [2009] I-3961.

[17]Paragraph 54.

[18]Paragraph 57.

apply.[19] It is also worth noting that the internal economy of each Regulation imposes its own concern. As regards conflict of laws, the demarcation between contractual and non-contractual follows along the lines of the scope of the Rome I and Rome II Regulations. Hence a matter will principally either fall under either one Regulation or the other. Brussels I, by contrast, features a default rule (Article 4) that covers matters that fall neither under 7(1) nor 7(2).

Another difficulty is the classification of obligations towards a third party. In *Handte*,[20] the Court interpreted Article 5(1) of the Brussels Convention as requiring an obligation freely assumed by one party towards another as meaning that 'it does not apply to an action between a sub-buyer of goods and the manufacturer, who is not the seller, relating to defects in those goods or to their unsuitability for their intended purpose'. The reason was that the special rule for jurisdiction would not be 'foreseeable [...] and is therefore incompatible with the principle of legal certainty'.[21] Other cases, such as *Réunion européenne*[22] and *Henkel*,[23] confirm this approach and, although it cannot be said for sure whether a direct contractual relationship (between defendant and claimant) is a condition for the application of Article 7(1), case law indicates a rather strict interpretation of the criterion 'obligations freely assumed by one party towards another'.[24] This could be in contradiction with the Rome I Regulation which applies to assignments and contractual subrogation by virtue of Article 14.[25]

4.4 Place of Performance Versus Habitual Residence of the Performer

4.4.1 Sale of Goods and the Provision of Services

Article 7 Brussels I Recast Regulation sets out a list of additional grounds for jurisdiction, referring to the specific subject-matter of the claim or specific disputes. For example, the special jurisdictional rule for contractual obligation (Article 7(1)(a))

---

[19] Briggs 2014, p. 265.

[20] Case C-26/91, *Jakob Handte & Co. GmbH v Traitements Mécano-chimiques* [1992] ECR I-3967.

[21] Paragraph 19.

[22] Case C-51/97 *Réunion européenne SA and Others v Spliethoff's Bevrachtingskantoor BV* [1998] ECR I-6511 (claim for compensation by the consignee or insurer of the goods).

[23] Case C-167/00 *Verein für Konsumenteninformation v Henkel* [2002] I-8111.

[24] Pertegás 2004, p. 179.

[25] For third party effects of the assignment of a claim, see Case C-548/18, *BGL BNP Paribas SA* [2019] ECLI:EU:C:2019:848. For consumer representative actions, see under 3.5.4. For assignment of consumer claims under the Brussels I Regulation, see under 8.5.2. For a subrogated employer, see C-340/16 *Kabeg* [2017] ECLI:EU:C:2017:576 (statutory assignee can directly act against the insurer of a vehicle involved in an accident).

reflects the proximity between the contract and the court. It provides that in matters relating to a contract, a person domiciled in a Member State may also be sued in the courts of the 'place of performance' of the obligation in question. Lit.b specifies for the sale of goods that, by default, this will be the place where, under the contract, the goods were delivered or should have been delivered. As regards the provision of services, the place is relevant where the services were provided or should have been provided. Residual cases fall under lit.a.

The connecting factor is different under Article 4(1) Rome I, which does not focus on procedural aspects but considers the habitual residence of the performer relevant. Thus, EU conflict of laws privileges the seller who will usually see his home law applied. The result is a divergence of *forum* and *ius* in cases where the place of performance is not located in the country of the performer. Of course, this will not necessarily thwart a course of horizontal conceptualisation with respect to the term 'provision of services' and 'sale of goods', an approach which is envisaged by Recital 17 of the Rome I Regulation, stating that these concepts 'should be interpreted in the same way [...] in so far as sale of goods and provision of services are covered by that [Brussels I] Regulation'. There may also be good arguments to draw assistance from the Brussels I Recast Regulation to interpret 'obligations arising out of the contract have to be or have been performed' as contained in Article 9(3) of the Rome I Regulation.[26] At the same time, however, Recital 17 explains in its second sentence that franchise and distribution contracts, although contracts of services, are exempted from the demand of coherence since they are subject to specific rules. Given that the Court of Justice has increasingly been confronted with the task to delimit sales from service contracts in the context of the Brussels I Regulation and given the challenges which have then arisen to qualify as mixed contracts,[27] problems of categorisation under the specific system of Article 4 of the Rome I Regulation are likely to occur.

4.4.2 Place of Performance: Autonomous Definition

The special jurisdictional rule for contractual obligation reflects the proximity between the contract and the court. Article 7(1) sets out that in matters relating to a contract, a person domiciled in a Member State may also be sued in the courts of the 'place of performance of the obligation' in question. For a general understanding of this provision it is important to highlight that the term 'matters relating to

[26]Crawford and Carruthers 2014, p. 9 (considering that "it would seem perverse for a judge vested with special jurisdiction in contract under Article 7.1.b to conclude for choice of law purposes under Article 9.3 of Rome I, that 'the law of the country where the obligations arising out of the contract have to be or have been performed' was other than the place of delivery of goods, or provision of services, as appropriate").

[27]Lein 2008, pp. 194–195.

a contract' refers to an obligation, freely assumed by one party towards another. Where the obligation was not *freely assumed*, hence promissory, it will fall under the special jurisdiction for matters relating to tort, delict, or quasi-delict (Article 7 (2)).[28] Having a wide scope, Article 7(1) also comprises situations where the existence of a contract is controversial or where a party has failed to comply with a contractual obligation.[29] The courts for the place of performance of the obligation (in dispute) have jurisdiction. It is for them to establish the facts of the case because of the proximity to evidence. Furthermore, the place of performance-rule has the bonus of clarity and preciseness. The last argument was disputed under the Brussels Convention because its basic rule, which is now Article 7(1)(a), opened the possibility to manipulate the place of performance, for example, in the case of several independent obligations or where an obligation could not be qualified as having one centre of gravity. Here, the claimant would wisely plead for the breach of that obligation which would offer him the best jurisdictional advantage.[30] In some cases, the persistent application of the inflexible *Tessili*[31]-doctrine—the determination of the place of performance by the *lex causae*—could even lead to the result of transferring jurisdiction to a court which has no connection with the dispute, in particular, in cases of pecuniary claims. Another problem was that the court was burdened with the task of looking into the *lex contractus* to determine jurisdiction. These and other objections were taken into account by the drafters of the Brussels I (Recast) Regulation who introduced autonomous definitions of the place of performance of the obligation in question for essential situations of the sale of goods and the provision of services, now Article 7(1)(b). Article 7(1)(a) reflects the approach of the Brussels Convention for residual cases (para c).

In order to remedy the shortcomings of applying the rules of private international law of the State whose courts are seised',[32] the important connecting factor of 'the place of performance' is defined as the place in a Member State where under the contract, the goods or services were or should have been delivered/provided. The qualification of a contract may lead to difficulties in some cases; this also due to the fact that the relationship between lit(b) and lit(a) is by no means clear.[33] For the purpose of localising the competent court, the obligation which characterises the contract at issue needs to be identified[34] and several factors to be taken into account.[35] Nevertheless, once the qualification has been made, the autonomous definition of the place of performance, focusing on a factual criterion, is a

---

[28]Briggs 2014, p. 262, para 4.233.

[29]Case C-38/81 *Effer SpA v Hans-Joachim Kantner* [1981] ECR 825 [7].

[30]Briggs 2014, p. 262, para 4.243.

[31]Case C-12/76 [1976] ECR 1473—*Industrie Tessili Italiana Como v Dunlop AG.*

[32]Council Regulation (EC) on jurisdiction and the recognition and enforcement of judgments in civil and commercial matters COM(1999) 348 final, 14.

[33]Briggs 2014, p. 262, para 4.245.

[34]Case C-533/07 *Falco Privatstiftung and Rabitsch* [2009] ECR I-3327 [54].

[35]Case C-381/08, *Car Trim GmbH v KeySafety Systems Srl* [2010] ECR I-1255 [33].

convenient approach to localise the competent court. This can be seen not only in the case of service contracts but also with the example of a sales contract that specifies the place of delivery where courts for this place will have jurisdiction unless the parties agree otherwise. Where the place of delivery is not stipulated in the contract, the 'most suitable' place will be that of the physical transfer of the goods to the purchaser and/or the place at which the goods are handed over to the first carrier for transmission to the purchaser.

The Court of Justice held that in light of the requirement of predictability and proximity, 'the place where the goods were physically transferred or should have been physically transferred to the purchaser at their final destination is the most consistent with the origins, objectives and scheme' of the Regulation.[36] This was confirmed in *Electrosteel Europe SA v Edil Centro SpA*, where the Court made clear that the national court seised 'must take account of all the relevant terms and clauses of that contract which are capable of clearly identifying that place, including terms and clauses which are generally recognised and applied through the usages of international trade or commerce, such as the Incoterms drawn up by the International Chamber of Commerce'.[37] As regards service contracts, the Court held that when there are several places of performance of the obligation characteristic of the contract, the 'place of performance' must be understood as the place with the closest linking factor, which, as a general rule, will be at the place of the main provision of services.[38]

4.5 Direct Activity—Harmonious Interpretation

The consumer provisions of Article 17 Brussels I and Article 6 Rome I grant a jurisdictional privilege to consumers who conclude a contract with a professional (discussed thoroughly in Chap. 8). Party autonomy is restricted, and protective default rules are provided where no choice of forum or law has been made. It is striking that both Regulations set out territorial requirements which largely coincide. Pursuit of commercial or professional activities by the person/*professional* in the State/*country* where the consumer has his domicile/*habitual residence*, or at the very least the direction of such activities to that Member State/*country* or to several States/*countries* including that Member State/*country* is required (emphasis on the differences in Rome I added).

Recital 24 of the Rome I Regulation explains that the concept of 'direct activity' should be 'interpreted harmoniously' for the sake of 'consistency' between the

[36]Id. [60-61].

[37]Case C-87/10 [2011] ECR I-4978 [26]; on the delivery in several places, see Briggs 2014, p. 270, para 4.249.

[38]Case C-64/17 *Saey Home & Garden NV/SA* [2018] ECLI:EU:C:2018:173 [44].

Regulations. Interpretative guidance is given by the next sentence of this Recital, which refers to a joint declaration by the Council and the Commission on the application of the consumer contract provisions of the Brussels I Regulation (44/2001). It attempts to give legal clarity by stating that for Article 15(1)(c) to be applicable it is not sufficient for a business to target its activities at the Member State of the consumer's residence, but, in addition, the contract must fall within the scope of such activities. This is already stated *expressis verbis* in the relevant provisions of both Regulations. Interestingly, the Recital also explains that the mere use of a website will not be sufficient to trigger the application of the consumer protective rules, even though this website soliciting the conclusion of distance contracts and a contract actually being concluded at a distance will be a factor in the assessment.

In the famous *Pammer* v *Alpenhof*[39] judgment, the Court of Justice did not seem to attribute a lot of weight to this statement for the purpose of interpreting the Rome I Regulation, at least as far as it concerns the clarification of the declaration according to which a 'the language which a website uses does not constitute a relevant factor.' However, in the following *Mühlleitner v Yusufi*[40] judgment, the Court was explicitly asked to elucidate the concept of 'directed activity', which the Court did with the necessary prudence. Acknowledging the language of the joint statement, the Court nevertheless placed a focus on the legislative history and teleological arguments and concluded that Article 17(1)(c) of the Brussels I Regulation does not require the contract between the consumer and the trader to be concluded at a distance. In *Emrek*,[41] the Court made clear that a causal link between the trader's website and the conclusion of the contract was not required either. In both cases, the Court observed that such a requirement would be contrary to the objective pursued by that provision, which is the aim of protecting consumers.

Another reason why that joint clarification did not hold much persuasive authority, other than it being merely embedded in a Recital, is its peculiar origin as a result of the inconsistencies during the legislative process. It is very common to summarise the evolution of a legal act in the Preamble of a Regulation, which may serve as a record of the negotiations and provides an overview of the *travaux préparatoires*, invaluable documents for the assessment of legislative intention. However, the Parliament was not included in drafting the statement, which was published after the institutions had agreed on the final text, wherefore there is no reference to it in the Recitals to the Brussels I Regulation. Neither was it replicated in the Recast Regulation, post-dating the Rome I Regulation. It is noteworthy that Recital 13 of the Proposal for the Brussels I Regulation (44/2001) spoke of the

---

[39]Joint Cases C-585/08 *Peter Pammer v Reederei Karl Schlüter GmbH & Co. KG* and C-144/09 *Hotel Alpenhof Gesmbh v Oliver Hellerand* [2010] I-12527.

[40]C-190/11 *Mühlleitner v Yusufi* [2012] ECLI:EU:C:2012:542.

[41]Case C-218/12 [2014] EU:C:2013:666.

accessibility of goods and services in another Member State being sufficient to constitute an activity directed to that State.[42] In this respect, the declaration can be regarded as an attempt to correct this reading.

4.6 Conclusions

The genetic affinity and complementarity of the Brussels I Recast and Rome I Regulations suggest a systematic approach when interpreting legal terms common to both legal acts. Commonalities can be spotted at first glance. The overarching concept of civil and commercial matters bears the same meaning in both Regulations, and so do the important concepts of 'direct activity' or 'sale of goods'. The contractual concept differs, but it nevertheless shows a common core, which consists in a legal obligation freely assumed by one person against another. In most of the cases, a contract can thus always be called a contract. Yet, there are intriguing differences, some of which cast doubt on the desired congruence. Application criteria do not entirely correspond, and certain concepts are shaped by the underlying rationale of conflict of laws and procedural law, respectively.

References

Baetge D (1994) Der gewöhnliche Aufenthalt im Internationalen Privatrecht. Mohr Siebeck, Tübingen

Briggs A (2014) Private International Law in English Courts. Oxford University Press, Oxford

Crawford EB, Carruthers JM (2014) Connection and Coherence between and among European Instruments in the Private International Law of Obligations. ICLQ 41:1–29

Kruger T (2008) Civil Jurisdiction Rules of the EU and their Impact on Third States. Oxford University Press, Oxford

Lein E (2008) The New Rome I/Rome II/Brussels I Synergy. YPIL 10:177–198

Pertegás M (2004) The notion of contractual obligation in Brussels I and Rome I. In: Meeusen J and others (eds) Enforcement of International Contracts in the European Union. Intersentia Publishers, Antwerp, pp 175–190

[42] COM(1999) 348 final.

Chapter 5
Rationale

Contents

Abstract The Brussels I Recast and the Rome I Regulations have absorbed EU principles and adjusted their DNA to serve the internal market and the EU Area of Justice. Nevertheless, they follow different rationales and have their own genuine concepts of fairness. The rules on international civil procedure show the role they serve when they consider the interest of the parties to have access to justice and the perspective of the court in making an enforceable decision available. Procedural Justice demands a proper conduct of proceedings and the avoidance of conflicting decisions. The multilateral rules under the Rome I Regulation, by contrast, are animated by conflict of laws methods and focus on the delimitation of legal systems rather than aspects of procedural economy. Although it has shaken off some ideals of Savignian type conflict rules, the Rome I Regulation searches for the closest connection of national laws with the contractual relationship.

C. Schmon, *The Interconnection of the EU Regulations Brussels I Recast and Rome I*, Short Studies in Private International Law,
https://doi.org/10.1007/978-94-6265-367-2_5

Keywords International Jurisdiction · Conflict of Laws · Universality · Perpetuatio Fori · Savigny · Neutrality · Access to Justice · Procedural Economy · EU Integration · Mutual Trust

5.1 De Esprit des Lois

The amalgamation of private international law and EU law has led to a firm interconnection between the Brussels I Recast Regulation and the Rome I Regulation. Both legal acts are therefore potential reference points for interpretation (Chaps. 1 and 2). It is therefore no surprise that Recital 7 of the Rome I Regulation explains that the 'substantive scope and the provisions of this Regulation should be consistent' with those of the Brussels I and Rome II Regulations. Indeed, what would be more assuring than to always call a contract a contract?[1] However, it would be evidently inaccurate to claim that the desire for congruence allows for a transferral of procedural values into conflict of laws. The dictate to 'never separate the rules of law from the purpose for which they have been made'[2] equally applies to EU private international law, to which the Court of Justice has adopted an interpretative approach oriented towards the purpose of a particular legislative rule.[3]

Are system and scope comparable or are the concepts similar? How do the Regulations approach the struggle between legal certainty and equity? Is there a common core in terms of party autonomy? As pointed out in the Preface, this book attempts to find answers to those questions and to elucidate the interconnection between Brussels I Recast and Rome I. This chapter will take a closer look at the fundamental nature of those legal acts and hence will discuss the rationale of their rules, their design, and genuine perspectives. For reasons of space, this will be done without giving full account of the dogmatic foundations and all themes that animate conflict of laws and international jurisdiction.

---

[1]Haftel 2010, p. 761, para 6.

[2]Montesquieu 1748, Chapter VIII (*Qu'il ne faut point séparer les lois de l'objet pour lequel elles sont faites. Des lois Romainessur le vol*); cited by Lüttringhaus 2013, pp. 31–32. Cf., however, Staudinger, 'Ausgewählte Probleme der D&O-Versicherung im Internationalen Zivilverfahrens-, Kollisions- und Sachrecht' in Lorenz (ed.) *Managerhaftung*, Karlsruher Forum (2009) 41, 60.

[3]See, for example, Case 12/76 *Industrie Tessili Italiana Como v Dunlop AG* [1976] ECR 1473 [9]; Case 14/76 *De Bloos v Bouyer* [1976] ECR 1497, 1508 [9,12]; C-144/86 *Gubisch v Palumbo* [1987] ECR 4861 [8]; C-45/13 *Kainz v Pantherwerke AG* EU:C:2014:7, [18-19]. See also Pontier and Burg 2004, p. 5 (teleological approach has become the dominant method of interpretation in the realm of international civil procedure law).

5.2 Characteristics: International Jurisdiction Versus Conflict of Laws

The Brussels I Recast Regulation is the central body of EU international procedural law. It shows its procedural DNA in that it intertwines state interests to regulate disputes linked to its territory with the interest of the parties to have access to a court that conducts a fair proceeding. The Brussels I Recast Regulation is thus required to take into account the perspective of the court in making an enforceable decision available. It must also respect due process principles and consider the interest of both the creditor and the debtor to take or fight actions before a court of a country that operates within the most familiar (domestic court) or most convenient (avoidance of transactional and litigation risks) legal environment.

The Rome I Regulation, by contrast, is a modern conflict of laws instrument that specifies which law should apply to a specific legal relationship in contractual obligations. It is thus not concerned with the assignment of a dispute to the authoritative power of a state court but deals with the meta question of applicable law. In conflict of laws, the search for the applicable law in the conflict of laws can be animated by different methods, ranging from unilateralism to multilateralism to substantivism. It will suffice here to explain that depending on the school of thought, conflict rules can focus on finding the best law for a specific situation or represent certain state interests, such as a predilection of the *lex fori*, or fulfil social functions, and hence can have an interest in the content of the laws vying for application.[4] The rules under Rome I are dominated by multilateralism, as they begin the search from the legal relationship and assign it to a particular legal order by conflict of laws rules. It is all about the delimitation of legal systems[5] instead of regulating a certain legal relationship.

Certainly, supranational rules on jurisdiction could also be understood as bilateral 'upstream' procedural conflict rules, deciding upon the application of the actual national civil procedural law—from this idea results the term 'conflict of jurisdictions'. However, this would disguise that the court seised will only answer the question of whether it has jurisdiction, never whether another court has jurisdiction (apart from *lis pendens* situations).[6] If the court is competent to hear the case, it will apply the *lex fori* and typically not be concerned with the question of whether to apply foreign procedural law, and hence not be confronted with a 'conflict of procedural laws'. By contrast, a forum favouritism under conflict of

[4]For an introduction to the traditions, themes, and main arguments in the conflicts literature, see Shreve and Buxbaum 2012; for an overview of codification attempts, see Symeonides 2014. See also Lipstein 1981.

[5]Pfeiffer 1995, p. 207.

[6]Mankowski 2005, p. 869.

laws[7] can have detrimental effects as it may lead to forum shopping or 'pernicious acts of judicial localism'.[8]

5.3 Universality

Accordingly, the conflict rules of Rome I follow a universal approach. They have bilateral design and thus determine which of 'all' state laws (domestic and foreign) apply to the situation. The court will not give preference to the *lex fori* but will approach the case with the assumption that national and foreign laws are interchangeable. This demonstrates the spirit of determining the law best applicable for the specific situation when it first categorises contractual obligations and then asks for the law applicable to them. Any law determined by the Rome I Regulation will be applied by the courts bound by the conflict of laws rules, which are the courts of the Member States except Denmark.

By contrast, the Brussels I Recast Regulation does not provide a comparable degree of universality. Whilst the territorial scope of application matches and, due to the adoption of a parallel international treaty, even comprises Denmark, it cannot follow a *loi uniforme* approach as this is the case under Rome I. For its application, Brussels I requires a specific link to the EU national forum seised, such as the domicile of the defendant. Based on the principle of reciprocity, a concept that is inherent in the law of international civil procedure, rules on jurisdiction and recognition and enforcement of judgments are expressions of the mutual trust of the Member States in their jurisdictions. This concept realises state interests, mandating looking at cross-border cases not only from the point of view of the facts of the case.[9]

For the sake of completeness, it should be mentioned that the degree of universality differs with respect to agreements of the parties. Under the Brussels I Recast Regulation, a choice of forum cannot be stipulated in favour of a non-Member State and therefore cannot establish exclusive jurisdiction in the chosen non-Member State forum. In this case, the general and special rules on jurisdiction will apply.

---

[7]Prime examples of *lex fori*-advocates are modern unilateralists such as Wächter or Ehrenzweig.

[8]Shreve 2012, p. 6.

[9]Cf., Von Bar 1987, p. 310 (reciprocity is expression to think from the point of view of the State rather than from the facts of the case).

5.4 Temporal Perspective

Already the status of conflict of laws as a meta-question whose fate is connected with a court exercising jurisdiction shows that there is a difference of temporal perspective for the rules on international jurisdiction and conflict of laws respectively. On the other hand, conflict of laws is, roughly speaking, relevant from the start. It is a temporal perspective of the Rome I Regulation to determine the applicable law when parties enter into an agreement. The Brussels I Recast Regulation, by contrast, thinks of disputes and thus attributes importance to the moment in time when the parties and their roles—claimant or defendant—are defined.[10] This explains why the area of jurisdiction provides for legal rules that consider certain conditions the moment a proceeding is instituted,[11] such as general jurisdiction,[12] the possibility of the claimant to choose between multiple fora,[13] or the submission of the defendant.[14] After the court is seised, avoidance of manipulation will be guaranteed, and procedural economy, state interests[15] and the protection of the claimant will be respected in that this court maintains jurisdiction even if the facts on which the competence were based change at a later stage (*perpetuatio fori*). For example, the Brussels I Recast Regulation has a focus on the defendant's domicile at the time the lawsuit was filed. A change of domicile after the initiation of the proceeding will not disturb the competence of the court seised to hear the case. Conflict of laws, by contrast, lacks equivalent temporal arrangements, makes an early decision about the law applicable and often follows the relationship of the parties involved by taking into account a change of the relevant connection factor (citizenship, transfer of movables, and others), and therefore allows a law other than the law that pertained before the change to be applied (*le conflit mobile*).[16] Certainly, as regards the area of international contract law it must be noted that for the purpose of determining the habitual residence of the parties to the contract under Rome I, the relevant point in time is the time of the conclusion of the contract.

---

[10] See also Pfeiffer 1995, p. 113 (discussing the temporal perspective under the aspect of the exercise of state power).

[11] Neuhaus 1955, pp. 253–254.

[12] As provided in Article 4 of the Brussels I Recast Regulation.

[13] See, for example, Articles 7–9 of the Brussels I Recast Regulation.

[14] Article 26 of the Brussels I Recast Regulation.

[15] Löser 2008, pp. 52–53.

[16] This change of statute is to be differentiated from rules on the intertemporal scope of application.

5.5 Legal Categories and Concepts

The qualification in conflict of laws is different from qualification in international jurisdiction. The latter determines whether the court has competence to hear the case, i.e. whether the defendant is liable to be sued in that court. The claim as a whole is thus subject to characterisation, which may subsequently give rise to further questions of law. Consequently, conflict of laws provides far more numerous categories than the law governing international jurisdiction.[17] It has created a variety of legal categories dealing with matters of consent, performance, validity, incapacity, and burden of proof. A displacement of the applicable law is justified by exceptions based on public policy or (overriding) mandatory provisions. Within the scope of general jurisdiction of the Brussels I Recast Regulation, the process of characterisation is reduced further, for Article 4 extends to almost all claims in civil and commercial matters that may be asserted against the defendant. Rome I, in contrast, applies to contractual obligations only and its provisions always require identification of the subject matter.

There are several legal concepts that demonstrate the differences between the areas of conflict of laws and international jurisdiction (selected concepts are discussed in Chap. 4). For example, typical for a civil procedural law act, the Brussels I Recast gives significant authority to the concept of 'domicile' for the purpose of determining jurisdiction. It shapes, for example, the grounds for general jurisdiction, and whether the defendant is domiciled in a Member State will influence the applicability of the jurisdictional rules of the Regulation. By contrast, the Rome I Regulation prefers—typical for a conflict of laws legal act—the ostensibly more flexible concept of 'habitual residence' in order to determine the law applicable to contractual obligations. It is also for procedural reasons that the Brussels I Recast Regulation is interested in the place of performance of an obligation for determining the contractual jurisdiction under Article 7(1), whilst the Rome I Regulation cares about the place of the performer for determining the applicable law.

5.6 Neutrality

The Rome I Regulation follows the justice ideal of the conflict of laws instruments of *Savignian* character to a large extent. This type of conflict rule is principally detached[18] from material law objectives and accords foreign law the same

---

[17]Haftel 2010, p. 761, para 12.

[18]Sonnenberger 2006, p. 116; von Bar 1987, p. 405 (noting that necessary connection between the parity of laws and the detachment of conflict of laws from substantive laws); Cf., Neuhaus 1976 p. 43 (noting the necessity of conflict of laws to be somewhat bound to substantial law values). For theories and methods of conflict of laws from a historical perspective, see von Bar 1987, pp. 360–438.

importance as the *lex fori*; it seeks the application of the law where the situation has its 'seat', hence understands proximity as the search for the closest connection of national laws with the contractual relationship.[19] It can, however, already be pre-assessed here that the modern PIL rules under Rome I no longer leave it to national contract laws to provide for social justice but accomplish what is known as *ius commutativa* under contract law. The prime example is that of consumer contracts. Chapter 9 will discuss and demonstrate that the justice ideal of neutral rules that are separated from the purposes of substantive laws cannot be sustained in certain areas. Neutrality should not be understood as a concept of equidistance. The most important contracts under the Rome I Regulation follow the principle of characteristic performance and usually benefit the merchant, who may use standardised contract terms and is not forced to operate within a legal environment he is not familiar with.

The law on international jurisdiction follows a different ideal as it seeks procedural justice. It is interested in proximity to the *facts* to improve the quality of proceedings and to safeguard the sound administration of justice. Yet, Brussels I does not follow the principle of closest connection but, instead, grants additional grounds for jurisdiction where there are close connections to the facts (the struggle between flexibility and predictability will be discussed in detail in Chap. 6). The law of international jurisdiction is certainly neutral too, at least to the extent that it is not interested in the outcome of the case. Its application also does not depend on whether the dispute will be decided by the *lex fori* or not ('international fungibility of courts'[20]). Under EU law, it is assumed that all courts are equally capable of conducting a fair proceeding. Otherwise, there would be no procedural justice that could serve as a justification for uniform rules on jurisdiction, recognition, and enforcement of judgments.

5.7 Access to Justice

5.7.1 Conflict of Interests

The general *telos* of rules on jurisdiction is, however, quite different to that of conflict of laws: It focuses on the court's task of independently making an

---

[19]Von Savigny 1849, p. 28 ("daß bei jedem Rechtsverhältnis dasjenige Rechtsgebiet aufgesucht werde, welchem dieses Rechtsverhältnis seiner eigenthümlichen Natur nach angehört oder unterworfen ist"); Neuhaus 1976, p. 49. Cf., Kropholler 2006, p. 26 (discussing the differences between seat and closest connection). It should be noted that in this argument, Savigny was preceded by Wächter who focused on the legal relationship being a guide for the court to apply law. However, he adopted a *lex fori* approach and concluded that the court must always follow its own domestic law, see Lipstein 1981, p. 22.

[20]Geimer 2009, p. 37; Kegel and Schurig 2004, p. 374; Heldrich 1969, p. 180; Neuhaus 1967, p. 35.

enforceable decision upon a legal dispute between parties according to the law.[21] The Brussels I Recast Regulation has therefore installed a set of rules on jurisdiction, which provides for access to a court and serves the interest of the claimant to adequately assert and enforce their claims. These rules consider that a legal dispute is always the result of conflicting interests between both parties. Both parties are usually interested in being able to provide the court with evidence that supports their position and to bring forward arguments in a language they are familiar with.[22] The third relevant player is the competent court, which, as a neutral arbiter, will be interested in being able to establish the facts of the case. The Court will have interest to be close to the facts and consider taking evidence from a State in which the proceeding was not constituted as troublesome, since it complicates the presentation of documents, inspections, and hearings.

5.7.2 Procedural Economy

When interpreting rules on international jurisdiction, it must therefore be kept in mind that procedural rules require a 'certain degree of physical control of the forum country' over the parties or the dispute.[23] Considerations of genuine civil procedural law, such as the effective service of documents, efficient taking of evidence, coherent adjudication, accessibility of documents, geographical distances, or reasonability of legal costs, are to be taken into account. These criteria, as well as the existence of available *fora* (or at least one forum), have the fundamental significance of guaranteeing a fair trial, as required under the EU Charter of Fundamental Rights.[24] For this reason, the forum state may have jurisdiction on the basis of its strong connection with the party or its centre of interest rather than on the subject matter of litigation. The general jurisdiction at the defendant's domicile under the Brussels regime is a manifestation of this rationale.

Conflict of laws, too, considers the interest of the parties to have access to justice. However, the respective roles of the parties are not the core issues of conflict of laws.[25] Whilst the avoidance of superfluous proceedings is a key pillar of the Brussels I Regulation,[26] Rome I does not feature an equivalent to the counter-claim[27] jurisdiction or to the special jurisdiction for cases involving

---

[21]Neuhaus 1955, p. 229; Mankowski 2005, p. 871.

[22]Heldrich 1969, p. 115. See for other barriers related to the litigation in foreign courts Pfeiffer 1995, p. 81.

[23]Bogdan 2012, p. 101.

[24]For examples on the influence of the Charter on the interpretation of the Brussels I Regulation, see Gillies 2015.

[25]Mankowski 2005, p. 876 (noting that there cannot be a situation in which no law finds application).

[26]CJEU Case C-23/78 *Meeth v Glacetal* [1978] ECR 2133 [8].

[27]Mankowski 2005, pp. 867, 875.

multiple parties. Next, there is no concept in conflict of laws that corresponds to that of procedural economy. It is a special feature and a quality of procedural law that it cares about geographical distances, especially where cross-border transactions are involved.[28] However, EU conflict of laws is not free from economic imperatives either. There is a certain parallel to procedural economy in that conflict of laws considers effectiveness and access to (foreign) law.[29] The dominant provisions on party autonomy in the Rome I Regulation demonstrate that traditional conceptions of state jurisdiction and state power are modified to serve the practicalities of international trade. Many default rules, too, reflect the idea of reducing transaction costs. The performer-principle is economically sound, reflects the practicalities of the internal market and will often benefit both sides of the market. EU conflict of laws follows thus a utilitarian approach.

5.8 EU Principles

5.8.1 The Internal Market and the Area of Justice

EU PIL has the function of advancing the objectives of the internal market and creating a genuine intra-EU area of justice (Chap. 2). The design of the Brussels I Recast Regulation is expression of that goal as it realises a 'free circulation of judgments' in civil and commercial matters within the Union. Mutual recognition of judgments and harmonised rules on jurisdiction are justified by mutual confidence of Member States in their administration of justice.[30] For the sake of a harmonious administration of justice, concurrent proceedings and irreconcilable judgments are avoided by rules of *lis pendens* and related action.

A duty to recognise a decision without possibility of corrective or supervisory measures requires flanking measures, including the harmonisation of conflict of laws. The conflict rules under Rome I were thus created to increase the predictability of the outcome of litigation and to avoid forum shopping. They are animated by the idea of multilateralism, as unified conflicts law throughout the community (of Member States) should lead to an international harmony of decisions: following the doctrine of Savigny, conflict rules of general application should apply without the requirement of reciprocity and designate the same national law irrespective of the country of the court in which an action is brought (Recital 6). Within the European Union, the harmonisation of conflict of laws enjoys a special relationship with the harmonisation of substantive laws as the *raison d'être* of conflict of laws is the variety of laws with which market participants are confronted when entertaining a claim.

---

[28] Neuhaus 1955, p. 256.

[29] Mankowski 2005, p. 874.

[30] Recitals 6 and 26.

5.8.2 The Price of EU Integration

The Europeanisation process comes at a price. Mutual trust means blindly accepting and enforcing a foreign judgment at the will of the creditor. Without corrective options for domestic courts, procedural fairness and access to justice are under attack. The exequatur—the proceeding for the declaration of enforceability—forms such a corrective option. It was removed by the Brussels I Recast Regulation, which kept only the public policy exception.

The Rome I Regulation shows some remarkable properties as well. Although it determines the law applicable *ad intra* and *ad extra* and avoids the existence of two different sets of conflict rules,[31] its internal-market clause (Article 3(4)) gives effect to the mandatory rules of EU law in cases where all other elements relevant to the situation at the time of the choice of law are located in one or more Member States. Of course, even the conflict of laws rules of Savignian character allow for exceptions to the strict parity of laws in the form of rules protecting imperative state interests ('positive mandatory rules' of the *lex fori*[32]). However, the internal-market clause is a doctrine that ignores the parity of laws entirely as it gives effect to all the mandatory Union rules in domestic cases, and not merely to provisions, respect for which is regarded crucial by a country for safeguarding its public interests.[33] A certain discriminatory focus on intra-EU situations can also be seen in the example of overriding mandatory provisions under Article 9, which protects crucial matters of public interest of the forum country. The respect for provisions that are crucial for safeguarding the public interest also covers Union rules, for they are part of the Member States order. The rule of Union law can also be observed at the level of interpretation. Article 9(3) states that certain overriding mandatory provisions of the law of the country where the obligations arising out of the contract have to be or have been performed *may* be given effect. It is considered that the principle of loyal cooperation requires that effect *must* be given where this would otherwise result in unnecessary harm for the Member State concerned.[34] Another corrective option is formed by the *ordre public*, demonstrating that there is no value-blind formalism in conflicts of laws.[35]

5.8.3 Further Adjustments of Dominant Doctrines

There are several other examples demonstrating that EU conflict of laws has shaken off some ideals of Savignian type conflict rules,[36] which seek to apply the law most

[31]Bonomi 2008, p. 168.

[32]Von Savigny 1849, p. 276 (assuming that such rules would disappear over time).

[33]Article 9 of the Rome I Regulation.

[34]Lang 1999, p. 116.

[35]Von Bar and Mankowski 2003 § 7 para 258 ('emergency valve'), Id. at 48.

[36]A prudent analysis was carried out by Lehmann 2010, p. 255. See also Kühne 2005, p. 815.

closely connected to the legal relationship.[37] Although Rome I follows the idea of finding among all available national laws the best suited to the situation, it does not actually seek the application of the law where the situation has its 'seat'. The default rules under Article 4 are at best an abstraction of the 'seat' as they do not precisely identify the law with which the *contract* is most closely connected. What is sought instead is a close connection to a *country*,[38] and the Regulation assumes that this will be the country where the party required to effect the characteristic performance of the contract has his habitual residence. A characteristic performance-principle is established for contracts outside of the catalogue.[39]

Another example is the predominant role of party autonomy, which is a pillar of modern private international law models. Private interest-oriented rules serve the practicalities of the international market. Parties can choose a neutral or beneficial forum and a law that has no connection to the seat of the contractual relationship whatsoever (Chap. 7). In addition, the conception of neutral conflict rules as rules that determine the applicable law without regard to the content of the substantial law is modified by rules protecting the weaker party to a contract; here, parity of laws and neutrality are superseded by social-economic values (Chap. 9). A related substantive, outcome-oriented approach can be seen in choice-influencing decisions by the EU lawmaker, such as preference for fully harmonised rules over the interplay between fragmentation and conflict of laws to advance the free movement of goods and protection of consumers.

5.9 Conclusions

The amalgamation of private international law and EU law has led to a firm interconnection between the Brussels I Recast Regulation and the Rome I Regulation. Both Regulations have absorbed EU principles and adjusted their DNA to serve the internal market and the EU Area of Justice. Nevertheless, they still provide genuine rationales and they follow specific concepts of fairness. The Brussels I Recast Regulation shows its procedural DNA in that it intertwines state interests to regulate disputes linked to its territory with the interest of the parties to have access to a court that conducts a fair proceeding. It has a 'serving role' as it considers the interest of the parties to have access to justice. Turning towards the conflict rules under Rome I, they are animated by conflict of laws methods, which are interested in the delimitation of legal systems rather than aspects of procedural

[37]Von Savigny 1849, p. 28 ("daß bei jedem Rechtsverhältnis dasjenige Rechtsgebiet aufgesucht werde, welchem dieses Rechtsverhältnis seiner eigenthümlichen Natur nach angehört oder unterworfen ist"); Neuhaus 1976, p. 49.

[38]Briggs 2014, p. 550 (emphasising the difference to the approach of common law).

[39]The law of the state is relevant where the party that is obliged to effect the characteristic performance has his habitual residence (Article 4(2)).

economy. They have a bilateral design and demonstrate the desire to determine the law best applicable for a specific situation. Differences in their characteristics effect differences in terms of temporal perspective, characterisation, and concepts.

References

Bogdan M (2012) Private International law as component of the law of the forum: General Course. Pocketbooks of the Hague Academy of International Law. Brill Nijhoff, Leiden

Bonomi A (2008) The Rome I Regulation on the Law Applicable to Contractual Obligations: Some General Remarks. YPIL 10:165–176

Briggs A (2014) Private International Law in English Courts. Oxford University Press, Oxford

Geimer R (2009) Internationales Zivilprozessrecht, 6th edn. Otto Schmidt, Cologne

Gillies L (2015) Fundamental Rights and Judicial Cooperation in the Decisions of the Court of Justice on the Brussels I Regulation 2009–2014: The Story So Far. In: Morano-Foadi S, Vickers L (eds) Fundamental Rights in the EU: A Matter for Two Courts. Hart Publishing, Oxford, pp 219–237

Haftel B (2010) Entre "Rome II" et "Bruxelles I": l'interprètation communautaire uniforme du règlement "Rome I". JDI 3:761–788

Heldrich A (1969) Internationale Zuständigkeit und anwendbares Recht. Mohr Siebeck, Tübingen

Kegel G, Schurig K (2004) Internationales Privatrecht: ein Studienbuch, 9th edn. Beck, Munich

Kropholler J (2006) Internationales Privatrecht, 6th edn. Mohr Siebeck, Tübingen

Kühne G (2005) Entsavignysierung des Internationalen Privatrechts insbesondere durch sog. Eingriffsnormen. In: Lorenz S and others (eds) Festschrift für Andreas Heldrich zum 70. Geburtstag. Beck, Munich, pp 815–831

Lang JT (1999) Community Constitutional Law: Article 5 EEC Treaty. CMLRev 27:645–682

Lehmann M (2010) Auf der Suche nach dem Sitz des Rechtsverhältnisses: Savigny und die Rom I-Verordnung. In: Bernreuther J and others (eds) Festschrift für Ulrich Spellenberg zum 70. Geburtstag. Sellier, European Law Publishers, Munich, pp 245–261

Lipstein K (1981) Principles of the Conflict of Laws, National and International. Martinus Nijhoff Publishers, The Hague

Löser A (2008) Zuständigkeitsbestimmender Zeitpunkt und perpetuatio fori im internationalen Zivilprozessrecht. JWV, Jena

Lüttringhaus JD (2013) Übegreifende Begrifflichkeiten im europäischen Zivilverfahrens- und Kollisionsrecht. RabelsZ 77:31–68

Mankowski P (2005) Internationale Zuständigkeit und anwendbares Recht, Parallelen und Divergenzen. In: Lorenz S and others (eds) Festschrift für Andreas Heldrich zum 70. Geburtstag. Beck, Munich, pp 867–898

Montesquieu C-L (1748) De l'esprit des lois, new edn. 1871. Garnier, Paris

Neuhaus P (1955) Internationales Zivilprozessrecht und Internationales Privatrecht: Eine Skizze. RabelsZ 20:201–268

Neuhaus P (1976) Die Grundbegriffe des internationalen Privatrechts, 2nd edn. Mohr Siebeck, Tübingen

Pfeiffer T (1995) Internationale Zuständigkeit und prozessuale Gerechtigkeit: Die internationale Zuständigkeit im Zivilprozess zwischen effektivem Rechtsschutz und nationaler Zuständigkeitspolitik. Klostermann, Frankfurt/Main

Pontier JA, Burg E (2004) EU principles on Jurisdiction and Enforcement of Judgment in Civil and Commercial Matters. T.M.C. Asser Press, The Hague

Shreve GR (2012) Choice of Law and the Forgiving Constitution. In: Shreve GR, Buxbaum H (eds) A Conflict-of-Laws Anthology, 2nd edn. Lexis Nexis, New York, pp 330–340

Shreve GR, Buxbaum H (2012) A Conflict-of-Laws Anthology, 2nd edn. Lexis Nexis, New York

Sonnenberger HJ (2006) Internationales Privatrecht, Einl. IPR. In: Sonnenberger HJ (ed) Münchener Kommentar zum BGB, 4th ed., 10 Internationales Privatrecht. C.H. Beck, Munich, pp 5–365

Staudinger A (2009) Ausgewählte Probleme der D&O-Versicherung im Internationalen Zivilverfahrens-, Kollisions- und Sachrecht. In: Lorenz E (ed) Managerhaftung. Karlsruher Forum. VVW, Karlsruhe, pp 41–84

Symeonides SC (2014) Codifying Choice of Law Around the World: An International Comparative Analysis, Oxford University Press, New York

Von Bar C (1987) Internationales Privatrecht, Vol 1, Allgemeine Lehren. Beck, Munich

Von Bar C, Mankowski P (2003) Internationales Privatrecht, Vol 1, Allgemeine Lehren. Beck, Munich

Von Savigny FC (1849) VIII System des heutigen Römischen Rechts. Veit, Berlin

Chapter 6
Certainty and Flexibility

Contents

Abstract The Brussels I Recast Regulation and the Rome I Regulation accept the challenge of serving the interests of both legal certainty and flexibility. Their system works with objective type-specific connecting factors and a healthy relationship between default rules and exceptions to it. Both Regulations give a great deal of freedom to the parties to make their own case. However, there is quite a bit of divergence, too: The Brussels I Recast Regulation sets out predictable, hard and fast-rules as it must think of procedural economy and the protection of the defendant. It must also consider how to live up to the mutual trust principle in the EU Area of Justice. Rome I, by contrast, thinks of how to realise a conflict of laws rationale and how to answer the need of justice for the merit of an individual case. It

C. Schmon, *The Interconnection of the EU Regulations Brussels I Recast and Rome I*, Short Studies in Private International Law,
https://doi.org/10.1007/978-94-6265-367-2_6

cannot only set out a priori appropriate rules but needs to give a certain discretion to the courts.

Keywords Certainty · Flexibility · Party Autonomy · Owusu Case · Sound Administration of Justice · Closest Connection · Predictability · Discretion · Forum Non Conveniens · EU Private International Law

6.1 The General Tension

EU private international law aims at providing citizens with appropriate outcomes in terms of legal certainty, predictability and flexibility' (Recital 9 of the Rome III Regulation). Easier said than done as it is a challenge to strike the right balance between these targets. Looking at the law on international jurisdiction, predictability as to the outcome of the litigation can be achieved by creating a system of exclusive jurisdiction rules. However, such law design would find no approval as it would ignore proximity considerations and the interest of at least one of the parties. Instead, the EU lawmaker opted for the adoption of uniform conflict rules. In the realm of contractual obligations, this is the job of the Rome I Regulation, which also had to make a choice of whether to focus on predictability and the strict observance of hard and fast rules or whether to assign greater importance to the idea of flexibility and justice in the individual case.

The prominent principle of legal certainty is part of the EU legal order (Chap. 2) and was incorporated in all legal acts that make up the corpus of EU PIL. What it actually entails needs explanation in light of the Regulations' principles. The Court of Justice illuminated that legal certainty requires uniform rights and obligations and respect for the wording of the provisions.[1] It is clear that such a demand may run contrary to justice principles in individual cases.[2]

It is asserted that the 'struggle' between legal certainty, which concerns clear, equal, and foreseeable rules, and the idea of equity, which gives due weight to the circumstances of a case, is 'as old as the law itself'.[3] This chapter will consider how these values are balanced by the Regulations and whether one comes at the price of the other.[4]

---

[1] Pontier and Burg 2004, pp. 83–84 (providing for an overview of CJEU case law).

[2] Vischer 2015, p. 10.

[3] Neuhaus 1963, p. 795.

[4] Cf., however, Pocar, p. 344, who correctly observes that concurrent fora impede predictability. However, he seems to misconceive that this is not contradicted by Recital 11 of the Brussels I Regulation (now Recital 15), which explains that *rules of jurisdiction* should be 'highly predictable'. This Recital argues in favour of a predictable application and interpretation of all rules including the alternative grounds of jurisdiction.

6.2 Party Autonomy

Above all, both Regulations achieve legal certainty by respecting the declared intentions of the parties, which should have a great deal of freedom to choose the competent court and the law governing their contract.[5] Choice of jurisdiction and choice of law-clauses considerably reduce risks of conflicting decisions because the judge is, to a large extent, deprived of his right to take into account the circumstances of the case other than the party agreement. However, as is the case for any agreement, it will not always be clear what the parties had really intended, and questions of formal and material validity may arise. Furthermore, the freedom of parties is not unlimited. For example, the Rome I regulation limits freedom of choice by giving effect to mandatory rules in internal cases or where a party to a contract is considered weak in comparison to the other. Rules on overriding mandatory provisions and *ordre public* put private autonomy in chains for the sake of public interest. The Brussels I Recast Regulation imposes limits on the freedom of a party by giving priority to a particularly close connection between the litigation and a Member State or for the sake of protecting the weaker party. The idea of party autonomy and its limits will be discussed in detail in Chap. 7.

6.3 Procedural Certainty

6.3.1 The Perspective of the Defendant

The Court of Justice has given much authority to the principle of legal certainty in the realm of international jurisdiction: the plaintiff should be able to identify the court before which he may bring an action whilst the defendant should be able to foresee the court before which he may be sued.[6] This rationale was exemplified in the famous ruling on the case *Owusu v Jackson*[7] where the Court flatly rejected the *forum non conveniens* doctrine by referring to the objective of the Brussels Convention to strengthen the legal protection of persons in the Community, 'by laying down common rules on jurisdiction to guarantee certainty as to the allocation of jurisdiction among the various national courts before which proceedings in a particular case may be brought'.[8] The Court concluded that legal certainty requires an interpretation of jurisdictional rules in such a way 'as to enable a normally well-informed defendant reasonably to foresee before which courts [...] he may be

[5]Provided, certainly, that the parties are informed enough to make a conscious decision.

[6]Case C-125/92 *Mulox IBC* [1993] ECR I-4075 [11].

[7]Case C-281/02 *Owusu v Jackson* [2005] ECR I-1383; see also Case C-440/97 *GIE Groupe Concorde and Others* [1999] ECR I-6307 [23], and Case C-256/00 *Besix* [2002] ECR I-1699 [24].

[8]Paragraph 39.

sued.'[9] As the application of the *forum non conveniens* doctrine allows the court seised a wide discretion to decide whether a foreign forum might be more appropriate to decide upon the case, such a privilege would 'undermine the principle of legal certainty', which the Court recognised as the 'basis of the convention'.[10] Accordingly, such doctrine would undermine the legal protection of persons established in the Community and negatively affect the uniform application of the rules of jurisdiction.[11] The Brussels I Recast Regulation therefore seeks to avoid situations where the competent court is unclear or difficult to identify. For this reason, the 'place where the harmful event occurred' (Article 7(2)) cannot 'encompass any place where the adverse consequences can be felt'.[12]

6.3.2 The Perspective of the Court

Whilst the Court of Justice looked into the *forum non conveniens* doctrine from the point of view of the defendant, it used the perspective of the competent court to argue against a burdensome obligation of Member States' courts to conduct a comprehensive taking of evidence as regards the facts relevant to determine jurisdiction under Article 7 of the Regulation. In *Kolassa*, the Court of Justice observed that the sound administration of justice and the independence of the national courts require an examination of international jurisdiction in the light of all the information available to it, including the parties' allegations. Yet, it emphasised that the 'aim of legal certainty requires the national court seised to be able readily to decide whether it has jurisdiction, without having to consider the substance of the case.' In view of the fact that the national court, at an early stage, 'identifies only the points of connection with the State in which that court is sitting that support its claim to jurisdiction under that provision', 'a comprehensive taking of evidence as regards the facts relevant both to jurisdiction and substance' bears a risk of 'prejudicing the assessment of the substance'.[13]

However, it should be borne in mind that it is not for the national court or the national procedural law to simply decide on the scope of assessment in relation to disputed facts that are relevant to both the question of jurisdiction and the existence of the claim (double-relevant facts). The national court *must* assess the facts in dispute and all evidence available where this is relevant to establish jurisdiction.[14]

---

[9]Paragraph 40; see also C-26/91, *Handte & Co. GmbH v Traitements Mécano-chimiques* [1992] ECR I-3967.

[10]Paragraph 41.

[11]Paragraph 43.

[12]C-168/02, *Kronhofer v Maier et al.* [2004] ECR I-6009 [19-20].

[13]Case C-375/13 *Harald Kolassa v Barclays Bank plc* [2015] ECLI:EU:C:2015:37 [61-63].

[14]C-12/15 *Universal Music International Holding BV v Schilling et al* [2016] ECLI:EU:C:2016:449.

To the existence of a tacit contractual relationship, the Court of Justice held that its demonstration would require a 'body of consistent evidence'. It even went so far as to provide criteria which should be taken into account by the referring national court.[15]

6.3.3 The Sound Administration of Justice

The provisions on *lis pendens* are another example that the Court of Justice uses a relatively rigid and formalistic rather than functional method of interpretation. Rules preventing concurrent proceedings and irreconcilable judgments are necessary due to the specific feature of international jurisdiction allowing for cases in which several States may have jurisdiction in the same matter.

Driven by the spirit of international civil procedural law to facilitate the proper administration of proceedings[16] and to 'minimise the possibility of concurrent proceedings and to ensure that irreconcilable judgments will not be given in different Member States',[17] the Court of Justice understands legal certainty as a principle according to which the court seised in accordance with the Regulation should *a priori*[18] have the monopoly to hear the case. Where conflicts arise, for example due to a choice of forum clause agreed upon in a contract,[19] that court seised should decide on its own motion whether it has jurisdiction or not. The strict interpretation of the *lis pendens* rule under the Regulation 44/2001 has rightly been subject to much criticism. It ignores the legitimate expectations of the defendant and enables the claimant to make use of torpedo actions. This tension was, to some extent, met by the reform of the *lis pendens* doctrine under the Brussels I Recast Regulation, which provides that a court other than the court first seised is obliged to stay proceedings where it was not designated in an exclusive choice-of-court agreement.

---

[15]Case C-196/15, Granarolo SpA v Ambrosi Emmi France SA [2016] ECLI:EU:C:2016:559 [26-28]); cf., however, OGH 9 Ob 73/15y (Austrian Supreme Court) [2016] ecolex 2016,787 at 3.4 (national procedural law relevant).

[16]Recital 21 of the Brussels I Recast Regulation; Report on the Convention on jurisdiction and the enforcement of judgments in civil and commercial matters by Mr. P. Jenard [1979] C 59/1, 41.

[17]Recital 21 of the Brussels I Recast Regulation.

[18]Fiorini 2008, pp. 10–11 (noting that the Brussels Convention 1968 was, after all, finalised between the six founding States of the EEC, which all shared the same, civilian, heritage).

[19]Case C-116/02, Gasser v Misat [2003] ECR I-14693; see Fentiman 2007, p. 27; Nuyts 2007, p. 55.

6.3.4 Mutual Trust

The Court's strong focus on the uniform application of EU provisions rather than individual justice can be explained by the integration process that was made in the field of judicial cooperation, as well as the function of PIL to implement the four freedoms. The Brussels I Recast Regulation is a core legal act in the EU Area of Justice, in which legal decisions, authentic instruments, and court settlements should circulate without restraint. Its mission is to live up to the principle of mutual confidence in the Member States' judicial systems and to ensure a sound administration of justice. Having clear rules is certainly crucial for this purpose, and so is the avoidance of irreconcilable judgments and situations of non-enforcement. These objectives would be at risk if the Court exercised a broad interpretation of provisions that aimed at fostering that mutual trust or if it permitted discretionary power by national courts.[20]

Besides *lis pendens* provisions, this rationale is exemplified by the jurisdictional grounds for refusal of recognition and enforcement set out under Article 45 of the Recast Regulation or by the multiple-party rules under Article 8.[21] Rules that attribute special jurisdiction in certain cases must also be seen in the context of the sound administration of justice and efficacious conduct of proceedings. A multiplicity of competent courts 'heightens the risk of irreconcilable decisions', the Court argued in *Dumez*[22] and, similarly, in *Besix.*[23] The ties between mutual recognition and jurisdictional rules are also manifest in the context of the general grounds for jurisdiction under Article 4. As the Court held in *Denilauler*,[24] 'it is because of the guarantees given to the defendant in the original proceedings that the Convention [...] is very liberal in regard to recognition and enforcement'. The general jurisdictional rules thus 'serves as a counterpoise to the facilities provided by the [Brussels] Convention'.[25]

---

[20]See the statement in Hobhouse J in S & W Berisford plc v New Hampshire Insurance Co [1990] 2 QB 631 where the judge stated that "the availability of such a discretion would destroy the framework of the [Brussels] convention and create lack of uniformity in the interpretation and implementation of the convention; see, however, Kuipers 2012, pp. 30–31 (criticising that the Court is basically "adopting the same interpretation techniques with regard to PIL as it had done in the pre-Maastricht era to provisions of public law", instead of seeking to balance the interests of private parties).

[21]Pontier and Burg 2004, p. 37 ('The principle that judgments are to be fully respected has an influence on the interpretation of rules laid down in Title II of the Convention').

[22]Case C-220/88 *Dumez France SA and Tracoba SARL v Hessische Landesbank and others* ECR [1990] I-49 [18].

[23]Case C-256/00 *Besix* [2002] ECR I–1699 [27].

[24]Case C-125/79, *Denilauler v SNC Couchet Frères* [1980] ECR 1553 [13].

[25]Case C-220/84, *AS-Autoteile Service GmbH v* Malhé [1985] ECR 2267 [15]; see Pontier and Burg 2004, p. 56 (Article 2 is the cornerstone of the Brussels Convention and derogating rules must be strictly construed).

6.4 Flexible Conflicts Rules

6.4.1 Predictability

Similar arguments can be made to justify a formalistic reading of the provisions contained in the Rome I Regulation since it has the development of the EU Area of Justice, the coherence of Union law, and the sound administration of justice in mind. Recital 6 thoughtfully explains its nexus to the Brussels I Recast Regulation and the importance of legal certainty for the proper functioning of the internal market. It states that the Rome Regulation seeks to enhance predictability of the outcome of litigation in that the same national law shall be designated irrespective of the country of the court in which an action is brought; parties shall know upon entering into a contract what law will apply. The Rome Convention was created to put an end to the diversity of conflict-of-law rules in the area of contracts,[26] which were regarded as having distortive effects on the internal market. The integration of the internal market calls for the elimination of legal risks concerning cross-border business transactions and promotes the predictability of the outcome of legal disputes. This is the reason why the Rome I Regulation calls for a clear definition of habitual residence in Recital 39 by consciously avoiding the problems resulting from Article 63 of the Brussels I Recast Regulation, which established several criteria in order to determine the seat of a legal person (the concepts of domicile and habitual residence are discussed in this chapter).

6.4.2 Circumstances of the Case

However, the Rome I Regulation dissolves the dichotomy between the target objectives with mechanisms allowing the circumstances of the case to be considered.

Although the catalogue of objective connecting factors for eight types of contractual relationships under Article 4 ensures legal certainty, the Regulation gives the courts a certain latitude to determine the applicable law. Following Savigny's justice ideal of selecting among all available national laws the best apt to the situation, hence to find its 'seat', the connecting factors are not of a rigid nature but yield to the law of a country other than that which is indicated where it is clear from all the circumstances that the contract is manifestly more closely connected to that country. The underlying rationale of escape clauses is well-explained by Recitals 21 and 21, stating that the court should be awarded certain flexibility to respect the circumstances of the case, *inter alia*, where there is a *very close* relationship of the

[26]Report on the Convention on the law applicable to contractual obligations by Giuliano and Lagarde, [1980] OJ C 282/1; Preamble of the Rome Convention.

contract with another contract or contracts. The escape rules of the Regulation,[27] which give effect to the law of a country other than that which is indicated, are powerful instruments and demonstrate the importance of flexibility to avoid undesirable results. Their phrasing indicates, nevertheless, that these rules shall only be applied in the clearest of cases. A characteristic performance-principle is established for contracts outside of the catalogue. Recital 19 explains that a 'centre of gravity' approach must be taken when a contract consists of a bundle of rights and obligations which could fall within several contract types under Article 4(1).

Where the governing law cannot be determined by the default rules or the characteristic performance principle, the contract will be governed by the law of the country with which it is most closely connected. Recital 16 explains that legal certainty and foreseeability would be general goals but, nevertheless, the courts should have a certain 'degree of discretion to determine the law that is most closely connected to the situation.' Similar to the Rome II Regulation,[28] Rome I provides a flexible framework for conflict-of-law rules. That flexibility cannot be taken for granted is demonstrated by the Commission's Proposal suggesting conversion of the default rules into fixed rules, as they should be 'as precise and foreseeable as possible' to foster foreseeability and thus party autonomy.[29] Another rule granting the judge certain discretionary leeway to decide upon the applicable law can be seen in the form of Article 9(3) allowing certain overriding mandatory provisions of the law of the country where the obligations arising out of the contract have to be or have been performed to take effect.

6.5 No Jurisdictional Principle of Closest Connection

6.5.1 Proximity and Justice

Rules on international jurisdiction acknowledge that proximity to the facts can improve the quality of legal proceedings and the sound administration of justice. It is about procedural economy, access to evidence, and respect for the interest of the parties and the court. Accordingly, the Brussels I Recast Regulation distinguishes

---

[27] Article 3(4), Article 5(3), Article 7(2) subpara 2.

[28] Recital 14 of the Rome II Regulation: 'The requirement of legal certainty and the need to do justice in individual cases are essential elements of an area of justice. This Regulation provides for the connecting factors which are the most appropriate to achieve these objectives. Therefore, this Regulation provides for a general rule but also for specific rules and, in certain provisions, for an 'escape clause' which allows a departure from these rules where it is clear from all the circumstances of the case that the tort/delict is manifestly more closely connected with another country. This set of rules thus creates a flexible framework of conflict-of-law rules. Equally, it enables the court seised to treat individual cases in an appropriate manner.'

[29] Proposal for a Regulation of the European Parliament and the Council on the law applicable to contractual obligations (Rome I) COM(2005) 650 final, 5.

between certain types of jurisdiction as general, special, or exclusive in nature. It thus gives credit to the existence of close links between the contract and the court called upon to hear and determine the case. A multiplicity of potentially competent courts has an impact on legal certainty. It leads to predictability being understood as ensuring that the defendant can foresee the competent *fora* and that both the defendant and the claimant can rely on the availability of general jurisdiction in most cases.

A certain respect for justice in individual cases can be seen in the form of the jurisdictional rule concerning employment in different countries, to which the Court of Justice adopted a 'centre of activities' approach. Furthermore, the Brussels I Recast Regulation has introduced a noteworthy mechanism that allows the courts of the Member States to take into account proceedings pending before the courts of third States and then to decide[30] whether to stay or continue the proceedings, provided that certain requirements are fulfilled (Article 33). There are other manifestations of proximity in the Regulation which improve the quality of legal proceedings and the sound administration of justice. For example, the catalogue of exclusive grounds for jurisdictions are established due to a 'particularly close' connection between litigation and the Member State[31] (Article 24). The proximity thought is as strong as having the effect of depriving the parties of the choice of forum. It is considered that the courts of the *locus rei sitae* are the best placed, for reasons of proximity, to ascertain the facts satisfactorily and to apply the rules which are generally those of the State in which the property is situated.[32]

Similarly, the special jurisdictional rules under Article 7 reflect a close link between the court and the facts of the legal dispute.

6.5.2 A Priori Most Appropriate Rules

However, there is no *general* principle of *closest* connection in the world of international jurisdiction. In sharp contrast to Rome I, which points to a legal system that is, in an abstract sense, best suited for the case at hand and which provides for default and escape clauses, proximity to the facts only allows for alternative *fora* under Brussels I. Hence, except for the grounds for exclusive jurisdiction, the jurisdiction of the defendant's domicile will not be derogated by a *close* link between the court and the legal dispute. This reflects an objective of proximity that enables courts to hear and determine the case. Accordingly, in contrast to the Rome I Regulation (and the Rome II Regulation[33]), the system of

[30] *Arg*. "the court of the Member State *may* stay the proceedings [...]".

[31] Case C-412/98 *Group Josi Reinsurance Company SA v Universal General Insurance Company* (UGIC) [2000] ECR I-5925 [46].

[32] Case C-605/14 *Komu and Others*, EU:C:2015:833 [24].

[33] See for the relationship between certainty and fairness Dickinson 2010, pp. 127–131.

the Brussels I Recast Regulation does not provide for an escape clause; its rules must be *highly predictable* (Recital 15) to prevent the defendant from being sued in a court of a Member State which he could not reasonably have foreseen (Recital 16). The civil procedural provisions may be designed, *inter alia*, to 'confer jurisdiction upon the national court territorially best qualified to determine a dispute'.[34] Still, the Regulation offers no grounds for the Court to depart from a connecting factor because of a lack of close connection to the dispute.

As explained by Professor Jenard in his report to the Brussels Convention, the rules on international jurisdiction 'achieve a genuine legal systematisation which ensure the greatest possible degree of legal certainty' and 'determine which State's courts are most appropriate to assume jurisdiction, taking into account all relevant matters [...]'.[35] Similar words were used by the Court of Justice in the case *Effer Spa v Kartner*, where the existence of the contract on which the claim was based was in dispute between the parties. The Court made clear that the claimant can nevertheless invoke the jurisdiction of the courts of the place of performance, as the Convention conferred jurisdiction upon the national court 'territorially best qualified to determine a dispute'. Reference was made to the interests of legal certainty and the avoidance of concurrent litigation to interpret Article 5(1) of the Convention as comprising the competence to consider the existence of the constituent parts of the contract itself. Otherwise, the provision would be in danger of being deprived of its legal effect, as the defendant could simply defeat the rule by claiming that the contract does not exist.[36]

It can therefore be concluded that the jurisdictional rules under Brussels I are *a priori* 'most appropriate' and a derogation based on doctrines or factors outside the Convention of Regulation must be rejected.[37]

6.5.3 Foreseeability > Discretion

Consequently, within the scope of Brussels I, there is no room for a *forum non conveniens* where a closer link to a court of another country exists. Member States' courts have no discretion to determine a more (or the most) appropriate forum and cannot issue a court order preventing a party from continuing or instituting a proceeding before the courts of another Member State. It is irrelevant whether the court that issued the order was the court first seised or whether the court order is

---

[34]C-38/81 *Effer v Kantner* [1982] ECR 825 [6].

[35]Report on the Convention on jurisdiction and the enforcement of judgments in civil and commercial matters by Jenard [1979] C 59/1, 15.

[36]Ibid., para 7.

[37]Dickinson 2007, pp. 116–136 (offering an overview of the case law on the principle of legal certainty).

granted to restrain the defendant from pursuing a proceeding in breach of an arbitration clause.[38]

The tendency to give priority to clear, predictable rules over flexibility considerations is in line with the strong influence of the Brussels Convention by civil law traditions, which features a system of hierarchically ordered grounds of jurisdiction.[39] Special grounds for jurisdiction are considered a derogation from general jurisdiction and must therefore be strictly construed.[40] As the Brussels I Recast Regulation provides for multiple fora, it makes clear that the basic idea of rules on international jurisdiction is not to reach 'decisional harmony' (*Entscheidungseinklang*) but that it is driven by weighing party interests. Harmony and mutual trust are pursued by the implementation of a recognition and enforcement system and rules on pendency and related actions. It should always be predictable which courts are competent to hear the case. Once jurisdiction is established, a review can only be admissible in exceptional cases.

6.6 The Struggle to Achieve Justice

Where the values of predictability and proximity are badly balanced, situations of injustice may follow. A textbook example is the application of the inflexible *Tessili*[41]-doctrine, according to which, for the purposes of Article 5(1) Brussels Convention, the place of performance ought to be determined by the *lex causae*. In pecuniary cases, the trader was often granted a home-match, which subverted the idea of restricting a *forum actoris* to duly justified cases. More importantly, this could lead to the special jurisdiction of a court that does not have a connection to the dispute, let alone a close connection.

However, a request for flexibility in individual cases was rejected in another textbook case, the judgment on *Custom Made Commercial Ltd v Stawa Metallbau GmbH*,[42] where the Court favoured the foreseeability and spirit of the Brussels Convention over the purpose of the special provisions. The autonomous definition for the 'place of performance of the obligation' for the sale of goods and the provision of services introduced by the Brussels I Recast Regulation helped to put an end to these procedural 'distortions'. Yet, this and other cases, or the example of multiple criteria for the autonomous concept of 'domicile', show that legal certainty is a relative concept, and much will depend on the concrete design of the provision.

[38] Case C-185/07 *Allianz SpA v West Tankers Inc* [2009] ECR I-663.

[39] Fiorini 2008, pp. 10–11.

[40] Case 150/77 *Bertrand* [1978] ECR 1431, para 17; Case C-464/01 *Gruber v Bay Wa AG* [2005] ECR I-439 [32]; recently Case C-645/11 *Land Berlin v Ellen Mirjam Sapir et al.* ECLI:EU:C:2013:228 [41].

[41] Case C-12/76 [1976] ECR 1473—*Industrie Tessili Italiana Como v Dunlop AG.*

[42] Case C-288/92 [1994] ECR I-2913; C-440/97 *Group Concorde v Master of the Vessel "Suhadiwarno Panjan"* [1999] ECR I-6307.

For example, its neighbour-provision—Article 4 of the Rome I Regulation, is less troublesome. Although it provides for a closest connection-test, the rules are relatively firm and give attention to the habitual residence of the performer. This solution reflects the rejection of the procedural aspect of performance and the desire to foster legal certainty.[43]

6.7 Conclusions

The Brussels I Recast Regulation and the Rome I Regulation accept the challenge of serving the interests of both legal certainty and flexibility. They operate with rules on party autonomy, objective type-specific connecting factors and make provisions for a variety of different situations. However, there is quite a bit of divergence in how to solve the struggle between legal certainty and equity in individual cases. The Brussels I Recast Regulation sets out hard-and-fast rules as it focuses on procedural economy and protection of the defendant. It considers how to live up to the mutual trust principle in the EU Area of Justice. The Rome I Regulation, by contrast, thinks of how to realise a conflict of laws rationale and how to address the need of justice for the merit of an individual case. It cannot only set out *a priori* appropriate rules but needs to give a certain discretion to the courts.

References

Dickinson A (2007) Legal Certainty and the Brussels Convention – Too Much of a Good Thing? In: de Vareilles-Sommières P (ed) Forum Shopping in the European Judicial Area. Hart Publishing, Oxford, pp 116–136

Dickinson A (2010) The Rome II Regulation – The Law Applicable to Non-Contractual Obligations. Oxford University Press, Oxford

Fentiman R (2007) Parallel Proceedings and Jurisdiction Agreements in Europe. In: de Vareilles-Sommières P (ed) Forum Shopping in the European Judicial Area. Hart Publishing, Oxford, pp 27–54

Fiorini A (2008) The Codification of Private International Law in Europe: Could the Community Learn from the Experience of Mixed Jurisdictions? EJCL 12:1–16

Kuipers JJ (2012) EU Law and Private International Law: The Interrelationship in Contractual Obligations. Martinus Nijhoff Publishers, Leiden

Max Planck Institute for Comparative and International Private Law (2007) Comments on the European Commission's Proposal for a Regulation of European Parliament and the Council on the law applicable to contractual obligations ("Rome I"). RabelsZ 71:225–344

Neuhaus PH (1963) Legal Certainty versus Equity in the Conflict of Laws. Law & Contemp. Prob. 28:795–807

[43] Max Planck Institute for Comparative and International Private Law, 'Comments on the European Commission's Proposal for a Regulation of European Parliament and the Council on the law applicable to contractual obligations ("Rome I")' (2007) 71 RabelsZ (2007) 225, 237.

Nuyts A (2007) The Enforcement of Jurisdiction Agreements Further to Gasser and the Community Principle of Abuse of Right. In: de Vareilles-Sommières P (ed) Forum Shopping in the European Judicial Area. Hart Publishing, Oxford, pp 55–73

Pocar F (2009) Some Remarks on the Relationship between the Rome I and the Brussels I Regulations. In: Ferrari F, Leible S (eds) Rome I Regulation: The Law Applicable to Contractual Obligations in Europe. Sellier European Law Publishers, Munich, pp 343–348

Pontier JA, Burg E (2004) EU principles on Jurisdiction and Enforcement of Judgment in Civil and Commercial Matters. T.M.C. Asser Press, The Hague

Vischer F (2015) The antagonism between legal security and the search for justice in the field of contracts. Collected Courses of The Hague Academy of International Law 142:1–70

Chapter 7
Party Autonomy

Contents

Abstract Party autonomy rallies almost unquestioned support in international contract law. However, it is controversial to define the borders and parameters of party autonomy. Lawmakers have regulated party autonomy in international transactions by setting out conditions under which parties may choose the law which governs their contractual relationship or define a forum before which a claim should be brought. The same holds true for the Brussels I Recast and the Rome I Regulations, both of which respect the declared intention of the parties and implement restrictions that limit the choice of forum and law generally or for certain contracts. On a more granular level, the relevant rules pay tribute to the fundamental and distinctive characteristics of rules on jurisdiction and conflict of laws, respectively. The Rome I Regulation pays respect to all circumstances of a case and tends to review the result of a choice considering public policy. The Brussels I Regulation follows a procedural rationale when it provides a variety of options for forum agreements. If choices are made in contradiction with overriding principles, it invalidates the choices altogether.

C. Schmon, *The Interconnection of the EU Regulations Brussels I Recast and Rome I*, Short Studies in Private International Law,
https://doi.org/10.1007/978-94-6265-367-2_7

Keywords Party Autonomy · Contractual Freedom · Choice of Law · Choice of Forum · Commercial Arbitration · Limits of Party Autonomy · Validity · Universality · Internationality

7.1 Theoretical Foundations

7.1.1 Introduction

Under which conditions should parties to a contract be able to define a forum before which a claim should be brought in case of dispute, and under which conditions may they choose the law which governs their contractual relationship? Whilst such questions are commonly addressed by those who wish to breathe life into the EU provisions on private international law, only a few scholars dwell on theoretical justifications for party autonomy. Sympathetic to the needs of globalised commercial practices, the parties' freedom is so commonly accepted that many take it as for granted as the freedom to conclude contracts. Indeed, if persons are free to decide whether and under what conditions to exchange properties, it seems natural that they should also be free to decide which law should govern their contractual relationship and what to do if disputes arise.

7.1.2 Freedom to Contract

The sanctity of *private* autonomy under contract law results from the success of classical-liberal market doctrines. In their early forms, they speak of private individuals who should get what they want and give others what they desire. Then, as prominently concluded by Adam Smith, 'man will be more likely to prevail'.[1] In the language of the law, this methodological concept translates into rules that regulate the process of private exchange on the basic principle of *pacta sunt servanda*, such as which agreements to consider as legally binding, to define the rights and obligations created by ambiguous agreements, or to determine the consequences of a breach of contract.[2] The lawmaker also has to guarantee the enforcement of agreements. A court should serve as a neutral arbiter and not include terms the parties have not agreed upon. Rather than attributing importance to the actual outcome of the case, fairness will be achieved by ensuring that the processes in place are correctly followed and that they are free of flaws, such as

[1]Smith 1776.

[2]Specifically, which agreements shall be considered as legally binding, to define the rights and duties created by enforceable but otherwise ambiguous agreements, and to determine the consequences of a breach of contract; see Kronman 1980, p. 472.

misrepresentation and duress. The result of this approach, sometimes referred to as procedural fairness, has the advantage of legal certainty, as the law will not assess the adequacy of consideration of a contract. The determination of a *iustum pretium* is superfluous. Certainly, contemporary national contract laws follow a more social policy-oriented agenda when they provide elements of substantive fairness, which address, for example, a grossly inadequate bargain. Obligations to contract are expected to address discrimination, enable access to universal services, and are acknowledged in monopolistic situations. Another commonality of modern laws is the respect for the weaker party, who is not on an equal footing with a professional or who may be in need of special treatment due to a particularly vulnerable situation. Nevertheless, save for these and other exceptions, the principle of contractual freedom applies in all modern national contract laws.

7.1.3 Party Autonomy in Private International Law

Distinct from the concept of contractual freedom, which operates within a legal order that sets conditions and boundaries for private law, party autonomy in private international law operates between legal orders. It leaves the boundaries of contract law when it is concerned with the applicable law and the competent forum. There are legal-theoretical debates about the normative foundations of party autonomy in private international law and whether it provides a genuine basis or justification for it.[3] Common arguments in favour of party autonomy relate to its efficiency or general perspectives on the freedom of individuals. Some consider party autonomy, at least from an anthropocentric perspective, as a manifestation of the virtue of the individual's natural will, as postulated by Kant or other liberal philosophers.[4] It is not the ambition of this chapter to analyse epistemological perspectives, but it shall suffice to explain that a genuine conflict of laws concept of party autonomy was not reflected in classic statute theory. The genesis of conflict of laws shows that the first initiative was not launched before the mid-19th century, when Mancini anchored private autonomy in his idea of liberty. However, he referred to *private* autonomy to justify why parties should be able to freely select the *lex contractus*. Mancini hence failed to set out a legal foundation that would distinguish between freedom of contract in substantive law and freedom of choice of law in private international law.[5] The establishment of the parties' choice as a decisive connecting factor under conflict of laws also does not reflect Savigny's conflict of laws model, which relied on the 'fiction' of the parties' voluntary submissions to objectively identify the

---

[3]Basedow 2001, p. 32; Kegel and Schurig 2004, p. 653; Lehmann 2008, p. 382; Leible 2004, p. 485; Id., 2007, p. 41; Martiny 2006, p. 1, para 8; Maultzsch 2011, p. 63; McClean and Beevers 2009, paras 13-003; Mills 2019, p. 103; Wicki 1965.

[4]This view can, however, not entirely justify party autonomy for legal entities, see Mills 2019, p. 9.

[5]Nishitani 2016, pp. 300–344; id., 2000.

responsible forum[6] and the seat of the legal relationship.[7] Similar statements can be made for innovative U.S theories with their predilections for the *lex fori* (Ehrenzweig) or better law approaches (Leflar). One has to look at more recent history to find modern theoretical foundations for a concept of party autonomy that operates independently of the substantive laws.[8] Even though there are numerous objections[9] against it, the 'stopgap solution'[10] of party autonomy is a predominant idea of contemporary conflict of laws, which modified the traditional conceptions of state jurisdiction and state power.[11] The parties' freedom and thus the protection of their expectations is considered a general principle[12] which has found its way not only into Union law, where it serves the practicalities of the internal market and free movement, but also into a considerable number of international treaties.

The success story of party autonomy can be also be witnessed in the realm of international civil procedure, where it derived from the emergence of jurisdiction based on submission and a focus on procedural fairness. The economic globalisation of the 19th and 20th centuries has brought a shift from state-power-oriented to private-interest-oriented legislation and case law. It has led to the emergence of national and uniform jurisdictional rules that provide procedural autonomy for parties to establish jurisdiction, and hence to select a predictable, beneficial, or neutral forum.[13] Indirectly, autonomy in choice of forum enables parties to also choose among different (national) procedural rules and decide upon the applicable law. In the form of arbitration agreements, party autonomy may even offer an opt-out of state court proceedings and access to an 'auto-poetic, parallel, world of private justice'[14] that is distinguished by flexibility and confidentiality. A utilitarian desire for autonomy is seen not only in the institutionalisation of international commercial arbitration but also in the manifestation of the various alternative dispute resolution venues, including amicable settlements and mediation. In today's business customs, it is thus a common standard to include choice of law and forum selection clauses in international contracts. Through those clauses, parties increase

---

[6]Without postulating a complete parallelism between jurisdiction and applicable law (*keine völlige Identität*) Savigny considered both jurisdiction and territorial law as different sides of the totality of the local law (*verschiedene Seiten des gesammten örtlichen Rechtszustandes*), see Savigny 1849, pp. 77, 91.

[7]Von Savigny 1849, pp. 152–153.

[8]See, for example, Haudek 1931.

[9]Basedow 2015, p. 115.

[10]Famous comment by Kegel 1971, p. 255.

[11]Mills 2019, pp. 22–28 (providing an overview about competing perspectives).

[12]Leible 2004, p. 485; Id., 2007, p. 41; Maultzsch 2011, p. 60.

[13]The preliminary documents and relate publications to the Hague Convention on Choice of Court Agreements 2005 provide for further readings on jurisdictional agreements, see https://www.hcch.net/en/instruments/conventions/full-text/?cid=98 (accessed June 2019). For the historical origins of party autonomy in choice of forum, see Mills 2019, pp. 68–84.

[14]Watt 2010, p. 254. For the implications on conflict of laws, see Mankowski 2005, p. 891.

economic efficiency as they have early and, arguably,[15] reliable information about where and under which law their disputes will be settled.

However, when drafting PIL rules, it is controversial[16] to define the borders and parameters of party autonomy, such as the mode of expression, the requirement of factual connections between the contractual relationship and the chosen law or forum, the legitimacy of the choice of a non-state law, the protection of a weaker party, the grade of internationality, or how to address *ordre public* questions. It will be discussed below how the Brussels I Recast and the Rome I Regulations have encapsulated private autonomy.

7.2 Party Autonomy Under the Brussels I Recast and Rome I Regulations

7.2.1 Significance of Party Autonomy and Hierarchy

The parties' freedom is a key principle under both Regulations. The contracting parties are free to choose the law governing their contract (Article 3 Rome I) and are free to designate their preferred court (Article 25 Brussels I).

The first difference is the position of party autonomy in the Regulations' hierarchy. Under the Rome I Regulation, party autonomy forms the cornerstone.[17] It follows a liberal approach when it grants the parties of a contract the ability to choose their law for every kind of contract. By their choice, the parties can select the law applicable to the entirety or to only part of the contract. No reference is made to any substantial or reasonable connection between the chosen law and the contractual relationship as is still the case under certain national codes on conflict of laws. A choice of law can also be implied by factual circumstances of the case, such as the number of connections to different laws[18] or pre-contractual correspondence.[19] Another factor is the existence of an exclusive jurisdiction clause.[20] Amendments of agreements are possible at any time and are valid for both initial

---

[15]Rühl 2019, p. 4.

[16]Symeonides 2010, p. 514.

[17]Recital 19.

[18]Kuipers 2009, p. 1511. For the problem of ambiguity of choice-of-law clauses and to the relevance of implied choices, see Stone 2010, pp. 303–309.

[19]Plender and Wilderspin 2009, p. 144.

[20]This is emphasised by Recital 12, which, however, merely mentions an agreement in favour of 'courts or tribunals of a Member State'. However, it cannot *a contrario* be concluded that a choice of jurisdiction in favour of a non-Member State court will have no relevance when interpreting the will of the parties, see Garcimartín 2008, p. 67 (noting that the reason why a forum selection clause in favour of a non-Member States is not mentioned as an indicator for a choice of law would be due to the principle *id quod plerumquem accidit*. 'If the parties have chosen the courts of a third country, they will very likely litigate in that country, where obviously the Regulation does not apply').

and partial agreements. Any change in the law to be applied that is made after the conclusion will, however, not prejudice formal validity requirements under Article 11 or adversely affect third parties' rights (para 2). It is therefore the general rule under Rome I that parties can select the applicable law. Default rules are set out in absence of a party agreement and determine the governing law pursuant to the catalogue of conflict rules for certain types of contractual relationships (Article 4).

By contrast, the Brussels I Recast Regulation follows a different order when it recognises the general jurisdiction under Article 4 to be its backbone. The defendant's *forum domicilii* shall principally be decisive; derogations are provided by exceptions expressly provided in the Regulation.[21] However, jurisdiction in the defendant's domicile is not the most powerful principle to which other rules are subordinated. In line with Recital 19, which explains that, save for exceptions, the autonomy of the parties to a contract should be respected, Article 25 gives a great deal of freedom to the parties to designate their preferred court(s). Rules on the *lis pendens* and enforcement ensure the effectiveness of party agreements. In order to protect the legitimate expectations of the defendant and to prevent an abuse of rights by procedural manoeuvres such as 'forum shopping' and 'torpedo actions',[22] the court designated in the agreement will have jurisdiction and any court of another Member State must decline jurisdiction in favour of that court (save for courts which have exclusive jurisdiction pursuant to Article 24).

Although not clear from the wording, parties are free to exclude the jurisdiction of the court which would otherwise be competent (*forum derogatum*).[23] The chosen jurisdiction is only deemed to be exclusive unless the parties agree otherwise. Hence, agreements for the courts of several Member States are possible. Other variations are feasible too: parties may agree that only one party may choose among several courts

[21]This chapter will not deal with indirect choice of forum options, for example through choosing certain objective factors such as the place for the performance of the obligation in question under Article 7.

[22]A common and simple strategy to delay proceedings is to bring a claim before a court not chosen in the contract, preferably in a judicial system inclined to producing delays. The permissiveness of this practice has been confirmed by the CJEU. In C-116/02 *Gasser v MISAT* [2003] I-14693, an 'Italian torpedo' was used to utilize the advantage of the priority principle by submitting a claim to an Italian court (Tribunale Civile e Penale di Roma) although an Austrian court (Landesgericht Feldkirch) was designated to have jurisdiction by a choice of court clause. The Court dealing with the relationship between a choice and forum made in a contract and the *lis pendens* rule expressed the priority of the *lis pendens* rule over choice of court agreements and held that only the court first seised is the competent court to decide whether it has jurisdiction, while the court second seised must stay proceedings until the court first seised has declared that it has no jurisdiction. For an overview on provisional and protective measures against torpedo actions, see Carl 2007.

[23]For the scope of jurisdictional agreements in detail, see Garcimartin 2015, pp. 280–282.

(asymmetric agreements[24]) or they may agree on a reciprocal clause stipulating that parties may only bring action in their own jurisdiction (excluding the general jurisdiction) or before the courts of the Member State where the other party is domiciled (excluding alternative grounds for jurisdiction). A jurisdictional agreement does not require any particular connection between the dispute and the forum state. Article 25 makes clear that a choice of forum agreement will fall under the Recast Regulation even when none of the parties have their domicile in a Member State ('regardless of their domicile'). Although not indicated by Article 6,[25] the same must hold true for the scope of application of jurisdiction by appearance provision that hints at the implicit choice of law rule as laid down in Rome I: pursuant to Article 26, a court shall have jurisdiction if the defendant enters an appearance without contesting the international jurisdiction of the court. Yet, in contrast to a 'real' implied jurisdiction clause, it is not required that the parties declare their submission *en connaissance de cause*. A meeting of minds is presumed because of the 'idea that by entering an appearance before the court [...] without contesting that court's jurisdiction, the defendant is by implication signifying his consent to the hearing on the case by a court other than that designated by the other provisions [...]'.[26] Since entering an appearance triggers the consequences of Article 26 automatically, the purpose of process efficiency has been given priority over the true intention of the party.

Jurisdiction agreements are 'robust' and the procedure can be considered 'transparent', since the agreement will be examined only by the court before which the proceeding is brought, and objections to recognition (or enforcement) of the judgment cannot be raised on the grounds that Article 25 was violated (Article 45).[27] An essential aspiration of the European Union is to establish a genuine European area of justice in which judicial decisions are able to circulate without restraint. For this reason, even judgments contrary to a choice of court agreement delivered by the court of origin cannot be reviewed or challenged based on that violation but will be recognised *ipso iure*. The Brussels I Recast Regulation has kept the test of public policy, but the provision does not apply to rules relating to jurisdiction (Article 45(3)).[28]

---

[24]The French Supreme Court, however, considered one-sided agreements that give one party the right to bring an action not only before the chosen court but also before any other court of competent jurisdiction, as void at several occasions, see *Mme X v Rothschild* (2012), No. 11-26.022 (Brussels Regulation); *ICH v Crédit Suisse* (2015), No. 13-27264 (Lugano Convention). By contrast, in *eBizcuss.com v Apple Sales International*, the Court considered a hybrid-agreement that ostensibly provided for (more) predictability valid.

[25]Article 6 refers to the law of the Member State to determine the jurisdiction of the courts for defendants not domiciled in a Member State. It sets out number of exceptions that include jurisdictional agreements pursuant to Article 25 without mentioning Article 26.

[26]Case 48/84 *Spitzley* [1985] ECR 787 [15].

[27]Briggs 2008, p. 239.

[28]Article 45 provides a list of reasons for the refusal of recognition (and enforcement) of judgments relating to non-jurisdictional and jurisdictional objections.

7.2.2 Universality and Internationality

The schemes of both Regulations respect the declared intention of the parties, thereby expressing the importance of legal certainty and predictability. A difference is the degree of universality of the agreements. As the Rome I Regulation, typical for a Savignian conflict of laws type, creates a *loi uniforme*, a selection of any state law is permitted (Article 3). Other non-state rules such as the UNIDROIT principles, showing the regulatory interest in avoiding private legislation, can simply be incorporated by reference into the contract (Recital 13). The Brussels I Recast Regulation follows a different model when it implements the mandate of the Member States to order their courts' jurisdictions in accordance with the principles of reciprocity and mutual trust. Regulation of intra-EU situations is driven by state interests and cannot effectively regulate a forum selection stipulated in favour of a non-Member State. This asymmetric system is designed in a discriminatory way when it does not prevent a party from ignoring the bargain for a third-state forum and, instead, brings a case to a court that is otherwise competent under the Brussels I Recast Regulation.[29]

Both Regulations require the existence of an international element for their application. Purely domestic situations are excluded. This is clear from Article 1(1) of the Rome I Regulation pursuant to which it 'shall apply, in situations involving a conflict of laws.' Although not set out *expressis verbis*, purely domestic situations are also excluded under the Brussels I Recast Regulation. The preamble to the 1968 Brussels Convention speaks of the 'international jurisdiction' of courts and the Jenard Report on the Convention[30] explains that the Convention 'governs international legal relationships' requiring the involvement of an 'international element'. It also follows from the main purpose of the Regulation to harmonise the Member States' rules governing international jurisdiction and recognition of judgments within the Area of Justice that purely domestic cases are of no concern to the Regulation—in particular ensuring the functioning of the internal market. Recitals 3–6 of the Recast Regulation use the terms 'cross-border implications' and 'conflict of jurisdictions' and refer to Article 81 TFEU, which explicitly mentions measures 'improving and simplifying the system for cross-border service of judicial and extrajudicial documents', and 'the recognition and enforcement of decisions in civil and commercial cases.'

---

[29]Whether such a manoeuvre can be declined on *forum non conveniens* grounds is disputed. The Regulation is silent on the issue of non-Member State jurisdiction agreements wherefore some argue that this matter should be dealt with under national rules. Others argue for a reflexive effect to Article 25, hence, to allow a court to treat such a jurisdiction clause as though it was an agreement within the scope of the Regulation. The Recast Regulation has brought an update of the predecessor Regulation when it allows Member States' courts to consider proceedings pending before the courts of third States for the question of whether they stay or continue the proceedings (Articles 33–34).

[30]OJ 1979 C 59/1, 8.

The question remains of how to classify cases where the only international element is the parties' choice. The Rome I Regulation is relatively unambiguous when it gives specific instructions on how to deal with situations where all elements are located in a country other than the country whose law has been chosen. A choice of law is effective, but parties cannot escape the 'application of provisions of the law of that other country which cannot be derogated from by agreement' (Article 3(3)). In order to protect the mandatory rules of the law of the European Union, a corresponding internal-market clause has been created (para 4): a parties' choice of applicable law cannot 'prejudice the application of provisions of Community law, where appropriate as implemented in the Member State of the forum, which cannot be derogated from by agreement'. The clear wording of the criterion 'all other elements' entails that a predominance of connection to another country would not be sufficient; in fact, not even cases where most of the elements relevant to a situation are located in a country other than the country whose law has been chosen are governed by this criterion.[31]

The EU rules on international jurisdiction are much less candid: whilst the Hague Convention would consider such situations non-international (Article 1(2)), the Brussels I Recast Regulation is silent on this issue. Dogmatically, there are no compelling reasons why a choice of a foreign forum should be warranted in the domestic realm, where parties can rely on a homogenous legal framework and predictable places for non-biased dispute resolution. An EU-wide harmonisation is not inspired by the requirements of the Area of Justice with its focus on internal market requirements and mutual trust in the Member States judicial systems. Systematically, however, there is no indication within the Brussels I Recast Regulation that the connecting factor of a parties' prorogation will not suffice for its application.[32] The Court of Justice also adopted a relatively permissive approach, when it confirmed in the famous *Owusu*[33] judgment that the international nature of the legal relationship need not necessarily derive from the involvement of several Member States. The Court also did not hesitate to recognise an international link in *Maletic v Lastminute.com & TUI Österreich*,[34] where a co-defendant, the travel agency, was domiciled in the same country as the consumer-claimant whilst the operator was situated in another Member State.

---

[31]See also Rome Convention, Article 3(3): 'where *all* the other elements relevant to the situation at the time of the choice are connected with *one country only* [...]' (emphasis added).

[32]For more on the international element and the difficulties with cases involving third-states, see Report on the Convention on the Association of the Kingdom of Denmark, Ireland and the United Kingdom of Great Britain and Northern Ireland to the Convention on Jurisdiction and the Enforcement of Judgments in Civil and Commercial Matters and to the Protocol on its Interpretation by the Court of Justice [1979] OJ C 59/71, 21; Case 281/02, *Owusu v. Jackson* [2005] ECR I-1383; Frauenberger-Pfeiler 2005, p. 125 (for the applicability of Article 23 Regulation 44/2001 for cases where the designation of a foreign court is the only international aspect); Garcimartin 2015, pp. 285–286.

[33]Case C-281/02 *Owusu v Jackson* [2005] ECR I-1383.

[34]Case C-478/12 *Maletic v lastminute.com Gmbh and TUI Österreich GmbH* [2013] ECLI:EU: C:2013:735.

7.2.3 Limits of Freedom

Even though both Regulations grant the parties a good deal of freedom, several restrictions are implemented that limit the choice of forum and law generally or for certain contracts.

The Brussels I Recast Regulation principally accepts private autonomy. A doctrine of *forum non conveniens* is alien to its system that gives priority to predictability rather than flexibility in individual cases. However, it discerns two important groups of restrictions concerning either the protection of a close connection between litigation and the Member State or the protection of the weaker party: jurisdiction agreements and prorogation by voluntary appearance are of no relevance when it comes to the group of exclusive grounds for jurisdiction as set out in Article 24, which allow a departure from the general rules of jurisdiction because of the characteristics of the subject matter. For its application, it is enough that the subject of litigation is situated in the territory of a Member State. For example, for proceedings relating to a right *in rem* in, or tenancies of, immovable property in a Member State, jurisdiction is awarded to the courts of the Member State in which the immovable property is situated. As regards the protection of the weaker party, the Regulation sets out that in consumer, insurance, and employment matters, a forum selection (even if provided in a trust instrument) shall have no legal force if the agreement is contrary to the relevant provisions. A departure from the relevant provisions may only occur through an agreement which allows the weaker party to bring a proceeding in an additional court or one which is entered into after the dispute has arisen.[35] The latter option is justified by the assumption that existing information asymmetries between the parties will typically be reduced after a controversy has boiled up and parties will start to become aware of their rights and obligations. In a similar vein, prorogation by voluntary appearance in the proceedings overrides the jurisdictional privileges of the protected groups of persons. Until the entry into force of the Recast Regulation, it was remarkable that Article 27 assigned priority to the court first seised and allowed that court to examine its jurisdiction even in cases where a party approaches this court in breach of a jurisdiction agreement. The Brussels I Recast Regulation has put an end to the strict first-come-first-served-rule; instead, it upholds the autonomy of the parties.

Under the Rome I Regulation, restrictions come in the form of various geographical or substantial limitations to private autonomy. It has been discussed that in internal cases, hence where all other elements than the choice of law are domestic, the mandatory substantive rules will prevail. An additional clause extends this instruction to EU law-protecting mandatory provisions, thereby recognising the matrix of EU law with its internal market objectives. Whilst Article 3(3)(4) puts private autonomy in chains to meet the requirements of 'purely' internal or domestic cases, 'overriding mandatory provisions' (Article 9) and *ordre public*

[35] Articles 15, 19, and 23. Regarding the additional possibility for an agreement where both parties are domiciled or habitually resident in the same Member State, see Articles 15(3), 19(3).

(Article 21) involve an international element relevant to the situation. They bear in mind considerations of public interest. For this reason, they must be construed more restrictively than the expression 'provisions which cannot be derogated from by agreement'.[36] 'Overriding mandatory provisions' enjoy superior status as they protect matters of public interest of the forum country in such a way that 'nothing in the Rome I Regulation', thus neither party autonomy nor default rules, may restrict their application (Article 9(2)). They relate to 'provisions the respect for which is regarded as crucial by a country for safeguarding its public interests, such as its political, social or economic organisation'. An *ordre public* limitation is set out by Article 21. It provides that 'the application of a provision of the law of any country specified by this Regulation may be refused if such application is manifestly incompatible with the public policy of the forum'. Then, as is the case under the Brussels I Recast Regulation, the Rome I Regulation introduced rules to protect the interest of persons considered as the weaker party to a contract: There are 'geographical' limitations for passenger contracts (Article 5) and small-risk-insurance contracts (Article 7), where the parties may only choose the law of the country if a territorial relation with the chosen state exists. Employees are protected by rules, which generally safeguard the protection afforded by mandatory rules or the country where the employee habitually carries out his work in performance of the contract (Article 8(1)). Consumers benefit from a similar rule: a choice of law in consumer contracts is valid, but it cannot deprive consumers of the protection afforded to them by the mandatory rules of the country where they have their habitual residence (principle of favourability). Finally, domestic rules concerning the formal validity of contracts are respected where rights in *rem* in or tenancy of immovable property are involved (Article 11(5)).

The example of consumer contracts shows that both the Brussels I Recast Regulation as well as the Rome I Regulation are open to concepts of favourability. Jurisdictional agreements are permitted if they grant the weaker party access to additional courts. References to mandatory national rules under conflict of laws guarantee a home (law) match for the consumer. However, there is also a major divergence between conflict of laws and the law of jurisdiction: Rome I permits party autonomy but reviews the results of it. The mandatory law of the consumer's country will prevail if a choice of law points to a less protective law. The chosen law will prevail if the result of a choice of law is more protective. Its procedural counterpart, by contrast, aims to concentrate a proceeding to the benefit of the consumer and does not consider whether the chosen forum may be more convenient. The lawmaker did not make use of the option to permit any forum selection but deems a consumer-unfriendly prorogation as having the effect of giving the consumer an additional forum.

---

[36]Recital 37.

7.2.4 Formal and Material Validity

Both Regulations require a *consensus ad idem* concerning the agreement, and both permit implicit agreements under certain circumstances. Nevertheless, whilst the *lex (loci) contractus* (by virtue of Rome I) is relevant for the validity of a choice-of-law clause, formal requirements of a choice-of-court—and this reflects the procedural aspect of the agreement—are governed by the Brussels I Recast Regulation and are to be interpreted autonomously.[37] Procedural fairness demands that a party should not be considered as having easily forfeited his or her right to the default forum. Article 25 thus permits a prorogation of jurisdiction only if consent is made in (a) writing or evidenced in writing or (b) in a form which accords with practices which the parties have established between themselves or (c) in international trade or commerce, in a form which accords with a usage of which the parties are or ought to have been aware and which in such trade or commerce is widely known to, and regularly observed by, parties to contracts of the type involved in the particular trade or commerce concerned (para 1). What was controversial under the predecessor Regulation, is clarified under the Recast Regulation: in line with Article 5(1) of the Hague Convention on Choice of Court Agreements (2005),[38] Recital 20 explains that—and this reflects the contractual aspect of the agreement—whether a jurisdiction agreement is null and void as to its substantive validity will be determined under the law of the Member State designated in the jurisdiction agreement. The doctrine of *renvoi* applies.[39] Another textual change is that the validity of the agreement conferring jurisdiction cannot be contested solely on the grounds that the contract is not valid (para 5, last sentence). Considering the consequences an agreement on jurisdiction may have on the position of the parties to the action, the Court of Justice has adopted a quite strict approach when interpreting the requirements of forum selection. For example, a clause that stipulates jurisdiction in the general conditions of sale on the back of the contract will only be effective if this contract signed by the parties contains an express reference to those general conditions.[40] On the other hand, the Court has shown some flexibility in cases where it would be a breach of good faith to invoke the invalidity of a jurisdiction clause.[41]

---

[37] Case C-214/89 *Powell v Duffryn* [1992] ECR I-1745 [14].

[38] For the relationship between the Hague Convention and the Brussels I Recast Regulation, see Garcimartin 2015, p. 284; for the relationship between Brussels I, Hague, and Lugano, see Hartley 2013, pp. 105–126.

[39] Agreements on the choice of courts are of no concern of the Rome I Regulation (Article 1(2)(e)).

[40] Case C-24/76 *Salotti v RÜWA Polstereimaschinen GmbH* [1976] ECR 1831; Case C 222/15 *Hőszig v Alstom Power* [2016] ECLI:EU:C:2016:525 [40].

[41] Case C-221/84 *Berghoefer v ASA SA* [1985] ECR 2699.

Like the Brussels I Recast Regulation,[42] the Rome I Regulation has set out rules to ensure that parties have given their consent. However, unlike its procedural sister, Rome I contains no requirement of the choice of applicable law being expressed in writing. A choice can be made expressly or clearly demonstrated by the terms of the contract or the circumstances of the case, and the parties can select the law applicable to the entirety or to only a part of the contract (Article 3(1)). The provision's design also betrays that Rome I favours upholding a choice of law, as it establishes five possibilities where such a clause could be valid.[43] A choice of law must satisfy the formal requirements of the putative applicable law, the *lex loci contractus*, in case both parties or their agents are in the same country at the time of its conclusion, or the law of habitual residence of either party, or the law of either of the countries if either of the parties or their agent is present at the time of conclusion (Article 11). Rome I thus refrained from imposing any particular restrictions as to the form of a choice of law. A choice of law is valid as long as a consensus can be found. Another interesting feature is provided by Article 10(2), pursuant to which a party may, in order to establish that he did not consent, rely upon the law of the country in which he has his habitual residence if it appears from the circumstances that it would not be reasonable to determine the effect of his conduct (para 2).

The different prerequisites concerning the formal validity of a choice of court clause on the one hand and a choice of law clause on the other hand could lead to the latter being upheld while the prorogation of the forum is invalid, although both clauses might be contained in the same contract.[44] Setting aside the differences concerning form and content and focusing on practical contract management instead, one can nevertheless recognise the interconnection between a choice of forum and a choice of law. In everyday business, such clauses can be found within the same contract, and in many cases, directed to establish a parallelism between the competent court and the applicable law, which would otherwise not be achieved.[45] Unsurprisingly, although the maxim *qui elegit iudicem elegit ius* has not found entry in the Regulations, an exclusive jurisdiction clause in a contract will be a decisive factor to be taken into account in determining whether a choice of law has been clearly demonstrated.[46]

---

[42]Case C-150/80, *Elefanten Schuh GmbH v Jacqmain* [1981] ECR 1671 [25]. Where the requirements laid down in the Regulation are fulfilled, such consent is indicated, see Mankowski 2011, Article 23 para 39.

[43]Kuipers 2009, p. 1510.

[44]Id., 1511–1512.

[45]Id., 1513.

[46]Recital 12, Rome I Regulation.

7.3 Conclusions

Party autonomy rallies almost unquestioned support in international contract law. It respects the will of individuals and serves the needs of the international market when it guarantees legal certainty and access to business-friendly venues for dispute settlement. The European Union follows this consequentialist approach and sets out liberal options for choice of forum and choice of law—which are often interlinked in contracts—in order to serve the practicalities of the internal market and free movement. Accordingly, in the Brussels I Recast and the Rome I Regulations, the declared intention of the parties is considered a cornerstone that requires no particular connection between the choice made and the contractual relationship. Both Regulations, with different techniques, put private autonomy in chains in favour of the mandatory regulation of certain subject-matters or to address public values.

On a more granular level, the relevant rules pay tribute to the fundamental and distinctive characteristics of rules on jurisdiction and conflict of laws, respectively. As regards the Rome I Regulation, this is demonstrated by an exclusive and universal design as well as by the way it pays respect to all circumstances of a case to determine the connecting factor of party autonomy. Rome I tends to review the result of a choice in light of public policy and other considerations but abstains from invalidating choices altogether. Its maxim is to respect the expectations of the parties, even though it shows certain discriminatory tendencies in intra-EU situations. The jurisdictional rules under the Brussels I Recast Regulation follow a procedural rationale when they provide access to certain *places* for litigation. Party autonomy thus opens the door for a variety of options, including non-exclusive or asymmetrical forum agreements. Other aspects are also imprinted by procedural ideas: Brussels I has the predictability of litigation and procedural farness in mind when it sets out formal criteria for a choice-of-court. If choices are made in contradiction with overriding principles, Brussels invalidates the choices altogether. Clear-cut rules thereby serve yet another purpose, which is procedural efficiency in the internal market. Jurisdictional conflicts should be avoided and mutual trust in the administration of justice fostered. These are the reasons why the true intention of the parties must give way in cases of jurisdiction by party submission and why jurisdiction agreements are 'robust' and not open for re-evaluation other than by the court of origin.

References

Basedow J (2001) Theorie der Rechtswahl als Grundlage des Internationalen Privatrechts. RabelsZ 75:32–59

Basedow J (2015) The Law of Open Societies – Private Ordering and Public Regulation in the Conflict of Laws. Brill Nijhoff, The Hague

Briggs A (2008) Agreements on jurisdiction and choice of law. Oxford Private International Law Series, Oxford University Press, Oxford

Carl I (2007) Einstweiliger Rechtsschutz bei Torpedoklagen. Internationalrechtliche Studien, Vol 50. Verlag Peter Lang, Frankfurt

Frauenberger-Pfeiler U (2005) Der "reine Binnensachverhalt", Art 23 EuGVVO und der öOGH. In: Bittner L and others (eds) Festschrift für Walter H. Rechberger zum 60. Geburtstag. Springer, Vienna, pp 125–138

Garcimartín F (2008) The Rome I-Regulation: Much ado about nothing? EuLF 2:61–79

Garcimartín F (2015) Prorogation of Jurisdiction. In: Dickinson A, Lein E (eds) The Brussels I Regulation Recast. Oxford University Press, New York, pp 277–311

Hartley TC (2013) Choice-of-Court Agreements under the European and International Instruments. Oxford Private International Law Series, Oxford University Press, Oxford

Haudek W (1931) Die Bedeutung des Parteiwillens im Internationalen Privatrecht. Springer, Berlin

Kegel G (1971) Internationales Privatrecht, 3rd edn. Beck, Munich

Kegel G, Schurig K (2004) Internationales Privatrecht, 9th edn. Beck, Munich

Kronman AT (1980) Contract Law and Distributive Justice. Yale L. J. 89:472–511

Kuipers JJ (2009) Party Autonomy in the Brussels I Regulation and Rome I Regulation and the European Court of Justice. 10 German Law Journal, 11:1501–1525

Lehmann M (2008) Liberating the Individual from Battles between States: Justifying Party Autonomy in Conflict of Laws. Vanderbilt J. Trans. L. 381–434

Leible S (2004) Parteiautonomie im IPR, Allgemeines Anknüpfungsprinzip oder Verlegenheitslösung? In: Mansel HP and others (eds) Festschrift für Erik Jayme. Sellier, European Law Publishers, Munich, pp 485–503

Leible S (2007) Rechtswahl. In: Ferrari and Leible (eds) Ein neues Internationales Vertragsrecht für Europa. JWV, Jena, pp 41–55

Mankowski P (2005) Internationale Zuständigkeit und anwendbares Recht, Parallelen und Divergenzen. In: Lorenz S and others (eds) Festschrift für Andreas Heldrich zum 70. Geburtstag. Beck, Munich, pp 867–898

Mankowski P (2011) Brüssel I-VO. In: Rauscher T (ed) Europäisches Zivilprozess- und Kollisionsrecht. Sellier European Law Publishers, Munich, Art 23

Martiny D (2006) Internationales Privatrecht, Art 3 Rom I. In: Sonnenberger HJ (ed) Münchener Kommentar zum BGB, 4th ed., 10 Internationales Privatrecht. C.H. Beck, Munich, pp 206–254

Maultzsch F (2011) Rechtswahl und ius cogens im Internationalen Schuldvertragsrecht. RabelsZ 75:60–101

McClean D, Beevers K (2009) The Conflict of Laws, 7th edn. Sweet & Maxwell, London

Mills A (2019) Party Autonomy in Private International Law. Cambridge University Press, Cambridge

Nishitani Y (2000) Mancini und die Parteiautonomie im Internationalen Privatrecht. Winter Verlag, Heidelberg

Nishitani Y (2016) Party Autonomy in Contemporary Private International Law - The Hague Principles on Choice of Law and East Asia Nishitani. Japanese Yearbook of International Law, 59:300–344

Plender R, Wilderspin M (2009) The European Private International Law of Obligations, 3rd edn. Sweet & Maxwell, London

Rühl G (2019) Choice of Law and Choice of Forum in the European Union: Recent Developments. 1 http://papers.ssrn.com/sol3/papers.cfm?abstract_id=1604615. Accessed May 2019.

Smith A (1776) An Inquiry into the Nature and Causes of the Wealth of Nations, Book 1. Chapter 2 Of the Principle which gives occasion to the Division of Labour. Penguin Books, London

Stone P (2010) EU Private International Law, 2nd edn. Edward Elgar Publishing, Cheltenham

Symeonides SC (2010) Party Autonomy in Rome I and II from a Comparative Perspective. http://ssrn.com/abstract=1697372. Accessed May 2019

Von Savigny FC (1849) VIII System des heutigen Römischen Rechts. Veit, Berlin
Watt HM (2010) Party Autonomy in international contracts: from the makings of a myth to the requirements of global governance. ERCL 3:250–283
Wicki AA (1965) Zur Dogmengeschichte der Parteiautonomie im Internationalen Privatrecht. Keller, Winterthur

Chapter 8
Social Justice—Consumer Protection

Contents

Abstract The Brussels I Recast Regulation and the Rome I Regulation acknowledge that the need for protection of the weaker party is even more pressing in situations that have a cross-border dimension. Both Regulations show their tandem function of protecting consumers with rules that are more beneficial than the general ones and set out almost identical preconditions for their application. In the realm of

C. Schmon, *The Interconnection of the EU Regulations Brussels I Recast and Rome I*, Short Studies in Private International Law,
https://doi.org/10.1007/978-94-6265-367-2_8

consumer contracts, the discrepancies between the procedural justice model under the Brussels I Recast Regulation and the conflict of laws justice model under the Rome I Regulation are reduced as social values under substantial law have been transferred into private international law. Save for exceptions, jurisdiction and applicable law can be determined by the same criteria, which will lead to a synchronisation of *forum* and *ius*. A mutual transfer of the Court of Justice case law across the legal acts will be possible. Due to different concepts and the application of a *favor defensoris* principle, certain frictions nevertheless remain.

Keywords Weaker Party · Consumer Protection · Alpenhof Case · EU Consumer Law · Brussels I Regulation · Rome I Regulation · Materialisation · Substantive Justice · Congruence · Favor Defensoris

8.1 The Weaker Party—Fundamentals

8.1.1 Asymmetries of Information, Experience, and Power

Modern laws recognise several categories of market participants who are considered relatively 'weak': employees, passengers, insurance policyholders, and consumers alike. Such persons should benefit from protective rules that consider the asymmetry of information, experience, or bargaining power between the parties. This chapter's focus will be on the protection of the consumer, who is typically less familiar with the subject matter than the professional and cannot easily comprehend practical or legal implications of agreements. Consumer law addresses information asymmetries and motivation disparities in business-to-consumer relationships (B2C). It is an expression of the welfare state model with its doctrine of 'consumer welfarism' that starts from the premise of an existing inequality between persons who depend on need-satisfaction and lack demand-regulation and persons who hold the bargaining power due to their economical superiority. From a social-economic perspective, the protection of the weaker party by way of transparency standards and protection measures against opportunistic or deceptive practices helps achieve a 'fair division of wealth among the members of the society'.[1]

There are numerous approaches[2] on how to best outweigh the imbalance between traders and consumers, depending on whether one follows a liberal market or co-ordinated market economy. Should the focus be on ensuring party autonomy and the functioning of the market, for example through transparency standards (market-rational welfarism)? Or should it be on the safeguarding of good contractual conduct, for example through unfair terms rules (market-correcting

[1]Kronman 1980, p. 472; for an overview of European social justice concepts in private law, see Micklitz 2011, 5.

[2]For changing paradigms and the consumer *Leitbild*, see Micklitz 2009, p. 419; Reich 2015, 326.

welfarism)? Another concept to look at is the main subject matter and interference in the exchange by rules on usury or *laesio enormis*. There is no need to dwell on the above-mentioned concepts, which all aim at outweighing the imbalance between parties.[3]

8.1.2 EU Consumer Law

Against the backdrop of the dynamics of transnational markets, the European Union[4] has legislated extensively in the area of consumer law. In EU contract law, market-rational welfarism seems to prevail. The benchmark is the 'average consumer who is reasonably well informed and reasonably observant and circumspect'.[5] It therefore follows a certain logic that a good deal of the legislative activity of the EU has been dedicated to realising what is referred to as the 'information paradigm', which intends to level the playing field between traders and consumers through provisions on information duties.[6] By contrast, the protection of disfavoured or particularly vulnerable individuals was traditionally considered a 'matter of the Member States in the scope of minimum harmonisation'.[7] This approach is reflected in 169 TFEU, which expressly refers to the right to information and which sets out a minimum-standard policy (para 2(b)) for measures that do not follow the internal market rationale (Article 114). Nevertheless, EU consumer law follows multiple protective purposes and ranges from transparency duties over protection from exploitation and psychological pressure to the protection of certain groups of consumers. To some extent, one can witness a departure from the information paradigm in favour of the 'vulnerable consumer'.

---

[3]For an overview of European social justice concepts in private law, see Micklitz 2011, 5. For the idea of achieving a fair balance of wealth, see Kronman 1980, p. 472.

[4]Abundant literature exists on aspects of consumer protection in the European Union, see, e.g., Reich and Micklitz 2014; Weatherill 2013; Devenney and Kenny 2012; Hill 2008; Lurger and Augenhofer 2008; Calliess 2006. For the relevance of behavioural insights to consumer protection, see Sibony and Helleringer 2015.

[5]Case C-210/96 *Gut Springenheide and Tusky* [1998] ECR I-4657 [31]; Case C-303/97, *Kessler* [1999] ECR I-513 [36]; Case C-358/01, *Commission of the European Communities v Kingdom of Spain* [2003] ECR I-13145, [56].

[6]For the information paradigm, see e.g. Reich and Micklitz 2014, pp. 21–22; for alternatives, see Busch 2016.

[7]Id., 45.

8.1.3 Cross-Border Protection

Although the problems encountered in B2C environments occur whether consumers act within their familiar legal system or outside of it, the need for protection of the weaker party is even more pressing when it comes to cases with a cross-border dimension. The growing participation of consumers in foreign markets, especially by means of electronic commerce, has massively changed the position of the individual, who is no longer limited to his country's border. However, whilst businesses may operate their product and financing strategy under various legislations, consumers, due to their economic inferiority, face substantial difficulties when leaving their familiar legal system. Consumers have no 'cost-justified incentive'[8] to learn about peculiarities of different jurisdictions, and often even blindly agree to terms of contracts with choice of law-clauses. Language problems may occur, access to information may be restricted, and the prospect of being liable under a foreign jurisdiction before a foreign court is typically a bigger issue for consumers than for professionals. The prospect of potentially long proceedings and insecurities regarding the availability of legal protection are strong disincentives for non-professionals to shop outside their home countries.

8.1.4 The Privileges Under the Brussels I Recast and Rome I Regulations

The need for cross-border protection of weaker parties is acknowledged in both the Brussels I Recast and the Rome I Regulation, which give jurisdictional privileges to insureds, consumers, and employees. Rome I additionally provides a protective rule for the carriage of passengers. As explained by Recital 23 of the Rome I Regulation, which is mirrored in Recital 18 of the Brussels I Recast Regulation, those persons should be protected by rules that are more favourable to their interests than the general rules. The Giuliano and Lagarde Report on the Rome Convention[9] refers to socio-economic considerations as the justification for protection.

The system of protection is similar: party autonomy is restricted, and group-specific default rules are provided where no choice of forum or law has been made. What differs are the design and scope of the relevant provisions: whilst the Brussels I Recast Regulation has a focus on weaker parties domiciled in EU States, the Rome I Regulation follows a universal approach. Design-wise, Brussels I subjects a derogation of its default rules to strict exceptions. Jurisdiction agreements at the expense of the weaker party are only permitted after a legal dispute has arisen. Rome I, by contrast, is more permissive. With respect to contracts for the carriage

[8]Rühl 2007, p. 37.

[9]Report on the Convention on the law applicable to contractual obligations by Giuliano and Lagarde [1980] OJ C 282/1, 25.

of passengers or small-risk insurance contracts, Rome I permits no less than five possible choices of the applicable law. A choice of law in consumer or individual employment contracts is valid, but it cannot deprive the consumer of the protection afforded to him by the law applicable by default (principle of favourability).

8.2 Consumer Contract—Article 17 Brussels I Recast and Article 6 Rome I

8.2.1 Negative Definition

Consumer-related provisions exist in both the Brussels I Recast and Rome I Regulations where the basis of a legal dispute is a 'consumer contract', a contract formed by a person for a purpose that is 'outside his trade or profession'. The negative definition of consumer is in line with EU consumer legislation and cannot serve as an argument for exercising a restrictive interpretation.[10] Both Article 17 Brussels I and Article 6 Rome I substantially cover all contracts between consumers and businesses, independent of the contract's subject matter. However, the consumer provisions apply 'without prejudice' to special provisions, and there are several specific types of consumer contracts which are exempted from the material scope of application.

Attentive readers will notice that the Rome I Regulation is more explicit than the Brussels I Recast Regulation when it clarifies that the contract must be concluded with 'another person' who is a professional and when it requires that the weaker party be a 'natural' person. However, Brussels I must be read in the same way: it can be derived from the purpose of protecting the weaker party that the contracting partner of the consumer must act within his trade or profession. It can also be extrapolated from the requirement of a weak economic position that natural persons rather than legal persons deserve general protection. This was confirmed by early case law, particularly the *Bertrand* judgment,[11] which also inspired the Schlosser-Report to the Brussels Convention, according to which only final consumers acting in a private capacity should be given special protection'. The Pocar-Report to the Lugano Convention explains in regards to the special types of consumer contracts for the (a) sale of goods on instalment credit terms and (b) for a loan repayable by instalment or for any other form of credit made to finance the sale of goods, that a clarification was not necessary as 'it is difficult to imagine that the

[10] Cf., however, Case C-464/01 *Gruber v Bay Wa AG* [2005] ECR I-439 [43] (negative turn supports a restrictive interpretation).

[11] Case 150/77 *Bertrand v Paul Ott KG* [1978] ECR 1431 [22]; see also Case C-89/91 *Shearson Lehmann Hutton v TVB* [1993] ECR I-139 [22].

seller/lender is acting outside the scope of a trade or profession'.[12] However, the Court's reference to the satisfaction of an individual's own needs in terms of private consumption should be considered a general rule rather than a specific requirement. Otherwise, many agreements characterised by a clear imbalance between the parties in terms of information and bargaining power, such as contracts on financial investments,[13] would not be covered by the protective provisions.

8.2.2 Consumer-to-Business Relations

A structural imbalance may also occur in consumer-to-business (C2B) contracts where a non-professional, natural person concludes a contract for the manufacturing of goods for a professional party or when such a person sells second-hand clothes to the professional. The exception for public take-over bids under Rome I may back up the opinion that such contracts are included.[14] Also, different from the Rome Convention, the Rome I Regulation and the Brussels I Recast Regulation both abstained from a reference to the demand side of the market. On the other hand, the idea of granting protection where a trader reaches out to the consumer's country (discussed below), does not quite fit to situations in which the consumer stands on the supply-side of the market. Also, harmonised substantial EU consumer legislation is traditionally characterised by a dualism of business/consumer and supply/demand of goods and services.[15] The Unfair Commercial Practices Directive, for example, makes it clear that it will only apply to unfair 'business-to-consumer commercial practices'. The Consumer Rights Directive explicitly defines sales and services contracts as contracts under which a trader transfers goods or supplies services *to* the consumer. Whatever the answer may be, the qualification of C2B contracts under the Rome I regulation will usually not have a large impact on the protection of consumers due to the performer-law principle and the fact that there are not many national protective rules for C2B contracts.

---

[12]Explanatory Report by Pocar (Pocar Report) on the Lugano Convention 2007 [2009] C 319/1, 80.

[13]That financial contracts fall under the general clause of consumer contracts is supported by the *exception* provided by Article 6(4)(d) of the Rome I Regulation, which excludes from its scope rights and obligations which constitute a financial instrument.

[14]Garcimartín 2008, p. 71.

[15]Mankowski 2006, p. 149; Calliess 2003, p. 352.

8.2.3 The Targeting Criterion

The territorial requirements[16] largely coincide and consist of (emphasis of the differences in Rome I added) a pursuit of commercial or professional activities by the person/*professional* in the State/*country* where the consumer has his domicile/*habitual residence*, or, by any means, the direction of such activities to that Member State/*country* or to several States/*countries* including that Member State/*country*. The focus on 'Member States' instead of 'countries' is in line with the different scope of application of the Regulations and the purpose of conflict of laws to apply universally; in sharp contrast to Brussels I, Rome I protects both EU and non-EU consumers. Another difference is the reference to the habitual residence instead of the domicile of the consumer. The reliance on two different undefined connecting factors puts unnecessary burden on the consumer to bring forward facts necessary to establish jurisdiction and applicable law. Article 19 makes clear that for the purposes of determining the habitual residence, the relevant point in time shall be the time of the conclusion of the contract.

Where the preconditions are met, both legal acts provide for comprehensive protection for the consumer by setting out protective default rules and by restricting party autonomy.

8.3 Default Protection

In the absence of a choice of law, the Brussels I Recast Regulation gives the consumer the right to choose to bring an action either where (s)he is domiciled[17] or where the defendant is domiciled; when reversing roles, the other party of a contract can only institute proceedings against the consumer in the consumer's country of domicile. Where the other party to the contract is not domiciled in a Member State but has a branch, agency, or other establishment in one of the Member States, that party will, in disputes arising out of the operations of the branch, agency or establishment, be deemed to be domiciled in that Member State (Article 17(2)). The Brussels I Recast Regulation brought a striking extension of the scope of application, granting the consumer a *forum actoris* 'regardless of the domicile of the

---

[16]Except for the special types of consumer contracts for the (a) sale of goods on instalment credit terms and (b) for a loan repayable by instalment or for any other form of credit made to finance the sale of goods.

[17]The Brussels I Recast Regulation determines therefore both international and national jurisdiction.

other party' (Article 18(1)). Counterclaims can be brought before the court in which the original claim is pending (Article 18(3)).

The Rome I Regulation calls for application of the law of the country in which the consumer has his habitual residence. Any law determined by the Rome I Regulation will be applied by the courts of all Member States, except Denmark, notwithstanding whether it is the law of a Member State. Where the scope of the respective protective provisions coincides, uniform interpretation would lead in most cases to a congruence of jurisdiction and applicable law, and thus, coherent protection under private international law would be granted to the consumer.[18]

8.4 Restrictions of Party Autonomy

Both Regulations set out restrictions of party autonomy in favour of the consumer. A forum selection before a dispute has arisen may not principally[19] have the result of depriving the consumer of the jurisdiction rules benefiting him under the Brussels I Recast Regulation. The 'hybrid' model of consumer protection under the Rome I Regulation is similar: a choice of law is valid but may not have the result of depriving the consumer of the protection afforded to him by the mandatory rules of the law of the country in which he has his habitual residence. The consumer may therefore rely upon the chosen law or his domestic mandatory rules, whichever is more favourable. The 'preferential law' approach strikes a compromise between the interests of traders and consumers: the first may choose the applicable law to the contract, the latter may rely on their familiar consumer protection standard. Depending on the contractual situation, professionals could be well advised not to include a choice of law clause when contracting with consumers. The favourability principle also comes at the price of parties and courts potentially finding it difficult to ascertain the applicable law. In this respect, the Brussels I Recast Regulation has the advantage of clarity: more or nothing.

Moreover, it may be difficult to decide on the question of whether a particular provision is a mandatory rule or not. As such assessment must be carried out in accordance with the law of the country where the consumer has his habitual residence, it could be difficult to ascertain the applicable law if it is not that of the *lex fori.* A deep dive into foreign law could increase procedural costs, which, in turn,

---

[18]Of course, numerous sources of law, dealing with EU norms on conflict of laws, contain provisions on consumer protection. For reasons of brevity and context, these will not be discussed here.

[19]Article 19(3) [The provisions of this Section may be departed from only by an agreement] 'which is entered into by the consumer and the other party to the contract, both of whom are at the time of conclusion of the contract domiciled or habitually resident in the same Member State, and which confers jurisdiction on the courts of that Member State, provided that such an agreement is not contrary to the law of that Member State'.

impedes access to law, as claims brought by consumers tend to be very small.[20] It would then be fair to also assume adverse effects on the business-to-consumer market. However, it is more realistic that courts will not always be willing or able to conduct a burdensome law comparison but will avoid the search for the dividing line between mandatory and non-mandatory law by applying the *lex fori* whether it is more favourable for the consumer or not.[21] In simple cases, the differences between levels of protection will be evident anyway—one may think of the length of legal guarantee period. Also, in cases where the consumer is sued or brings proceedings against the other party to a contract in the courts of the place where he is domiciled by virtue of Article 17 or 18 of the Brussels I Recast Regulation, the country whose mandatory provisions are the yardstick under Article 6 of the Rome I Regulation will usually be that of the forum.[22]

8.5 Rule-Exception Relation

8.5.1 Strict Interpretation of Special Rules

The case law of the Court of Justice on rules of jurisdiction is characterised by a strict interpretive approach with respect to provisions that constitute *leges speciales* in relation to the general rules. The Court has put emphasis on the rule-exception rationale of the Brussels system of jurisdiction and, even more, justified a particularly restrictive approach with the argument that the consumer protective provisions derogate twofold: from the jurisdictional ground for contracts and from the general ground for jurisdiction (Joint cases *Pammer* and *Alpenhof*[23]). The impact of a strict interpretation can be demonstrated by the often-referenced *Gruber* judgment regarding contracts of dual purpose. The dispute concerned the purchase of roof tiles for a farm building that was used for both farming (hence professional or, at least, related to professional) and residential (hence private) purposes. The Court held that (emphasis added) the claimant may not rely on the special rules of jurisdiction unless the trade or professional purpose is 'so limited as to be negligible in the overall context of the supply'. The Court justified this strict *de minimis* approach by referring to settled-case law according to which the jurisdiction at the defendant's domicile constitutes a 'general principle' and that rules which derogate from this principle are to be strictly interpreted. 'A fortiori', this would apply to the consumer protective rule under Article 14 of the Brussels Convention.

[20]Proposal for Regulation of the European Parliament and the Council on the law applicable to contractual obligations (Rome I) COM(2005) 650 final, 6.

[21]Basedow 2015, p. 416, para 628 and references cited there.

[22]Plender and Wilderspin 2009, p. 249.

[23]Joint Cases C-585/08 *Peter Pammer v Reederei Karl Schlüter GmbH & Co. KG* and C-144/09 *Hotel Alpenhof Gesmbh v Oliver Hellerand* [2010] I-12527 [51]; C-190/11 *Mühlleitner v Yusufi* [2012] ECLI:EU:C:2012:542 [26].

However, recent decisions are characterised by a permissive approach and emphasis on purposive arguments. When interpreting the 'directed activity' criterion, the Court held that Article 17(1)(c) of the Brussels I Recast Regulation does not require the contract between the consumer and the trader to be concluded at a distance (*Mühlleitner*[24]). In *Emrek*,[25] the Court made clear that a causal link between the trader's website and the conclusion of the contract was also not required. The Court observed that such a requirement would be contrary to the objective pursued by that provision, that is, the aim of protecting consumers, who are regarded as the weaker parties to contracts concluded between them and a trader (para 24). Consumers should not be dissuaded from bringing actions before their home courts due to problems in making their case (para 25).

8.5.2 Case Law: A Reconciliation Attempt

Whilst the classification of dual purpose contracts[26] hardly manages the balancing act between providing protection for persons 'for whom special jurisdiction is not justified' and those for whom it would be,[27] the judgments on the directing of commercial activities strain the rationale of the criterion 'falls within the scope of such activities' to its utmost. Traders are subjected to the jurisdiction of the country of the consumer's domicile in cases where consumers were not even aware of the website of the professional. However, the CJEU's rulings are far from arbitrary. The case law is characterised by the attempt to reconcile the need for protection of the weaker party and the commitment to avoid an extension of the scope of Article 17(c) of the Recast Regulation. For this purpose, it seems that the Court formalistically clings to the text and is reluctant to grant persons jurisdictional privilege where a situation is not positively covered by it. The exception shall not 'eat up the rule'. An extension to B2B relationships should be prevented by putting a strong focus on the private and final role of the consumer and by respecting legitimate expectations. Accordingly, and this is in line with the predominant principle of legal certainty under Brussels I, a multiplicity of jurisdictions (*Pammer*) should be avoided. A defendant should be aware at the outset before which court he or she may be sued. Predictability constitutes the 'foundation' of the law of international jurisdiction (*Gruber*). A *venire contract factum proprium* will be at the expense of the person who seeks protection.

---

[24]C-190/11 [2012] ECLI:EU:C:2012:542.

[25]Case C-218/12 [2014] EU:C:2013:666.

[26]The frequently used term 'mixed contract' should be avoided since, to use the words of GA Jacobs, there is "no such thing as a 'mixed contract'". Indeed, EU PIL looks at the whole contractual relationship and will qualify it as a consumer contract or not.

[27]Reich 2014, p. 324 (too narrow).

Thus, for proceedings brought by a professional assignee of the claims of a private individual (*Shearson*) or an assignee of consumer rights who is not acting within his or her profession (*Schrems*);[28] proceedings brought by a consumer association against a trader for using unfair terms in contracts (*VKI v Henkel*); proceedings concerning contracts for the purpose of future professional activity (*Benincasa*); proceedings concerning contracts that do not only have a purpose which can be regarded as being outside the person's trade or profession, hence where the consumer is to some extent on an equal footing with the professional[29] (*Gruber*); or proceedings concerning the claim for a prize that was promised without the *conclusion* of a contract (*Engler*,[30] *Ilsinger*), the specific protection sought to be afforded under the provisions is considered unwarranted. In turn, where the need for protection is clear, the Court seems to be willing to let a low standard for the application suffice. The Court does not demand the existence of a relative weakness *vis-à-vis* the professional (*Benincasa*), or that the contract is concluded at a distance (*Mühlleitner*). Consumers should not face difficulties making their case. Hence, procedural 'obstacles', such as burden of proof problems, should not dissuade consumers from bringing proceedings (*Emrek*).

8.6 Ratio Legis

8.6.1 Familiar Legal Environment

Both Regulations are inspired by the concern of protecting the consumer as the party deemed to be economically weaker and less experienced in legal matters than the other party to the contract.[31] Such persons should not be discouraged from shopping cross-border and taking actions if they see their rights infringed upon. In absence of a party agreement, consumer-friendly objective connection factors[32] seek to grant consumers their familiar legal environment: their local court will always be competent, and their local protective law level will always be granted.

---

[28]Case C-498/16 [2018] ECLI:EU:C:2018:37 *Schrems vs Facebook Ireland Ltd*. The Court focused on predictability and legal expectations of the other party to the contract to deny consumer protection for a situation where claims from a number of consumers were assigned to one consumer. See Schmon 2018, p. 248. Under conflict of laws rules, the qualification may be different since Rome I determines the applicable law at the time of the conclusion of the contract. It is not concerned with the roles of the parties (claimant or defendant) at the time the proceeding is instituted.

[29]Opinion of GA Jacobs, 16 September 2004, Case C-464/01 *Gruber v Bay Wa AG* [2005] ECR I-439, 40.

[30]Case C-27/02 *Engler v Janus Versan*d [2005] ECR I-471; for prize notifications in general, see Schmon 2009, p. 19; see also Zheng Tang 2010, p. 14 (considering the interpretation by the CJEU as too narrow because the inequality of litigation power justifies a protection).

[31]Recital 18 of Brussels I Recast and Recital 23 of Rome I.

[32]Kropholler 1978, p. 634.

With respect to the Rome I Regulation, the characteristic-performance approach, and hence the general preference for the seller's home law, is relinquished. Under the Brussels I Recast, the privilege for defendants (Brussels I Recast) and the proximity-based grounds for jurisdiction are abandoned, save for exclusive jurisdictional grounds. The fact that the 'commercial party is "fishing" for consumers' is a sufficient connection of the contract to the domicile of the consumer.[33] This shows that EU private international law (PIL) realises a genuine rationale of consumer protection.[34]

8.6.2 *Social Values*

Brussels I and Rome I also follow a regulatory policy of implementing social values from substantial law into PIL. It is a Treaty objective to ensure a high level of consumer protection (Article 169 TFEU) and EU consumer law seeks to 'compensate for the imbalance between parties in contracts concluded between a consumer and a professional'[35] and to protect the weaker party from exploitation. Consequently, EU PIL protects the weaker party whether or not this party is an active or a passive consumer[36] and regardless of whether this party acts in the role of the defendant or claimant. As this is the case under substantive consumer law, party autonomy is considered a tool of the stronger party to enforce his power over the weaker party.[37] Thus, a forum selection may only grant the consumer an additional forum; a choice of law may not deprive the consumer of that level.

The favourability principle of Article 6(2) of the Rome I Regulation illustrates that it is not (only) the proximity between the consumer and the applicable law but the 'substantive policy' which is the underlying justice model of this provision.[38] When the chosen law falls behind the substantive protection under the law of the

[33]Nielsen 2007, p. 315; see also Report by Professor Dr. Peter Schlosser on the Convention of 9 October 1978 on the Association of the Kingdom of Denmark, Ireland and the United Kingdom of Great Britain and Northern Ireland to the Convention on jurisdiction and the enforcement of judgments in civil and commercial matters and to the Protocol on its interpretation by the Court of Justice [1979] OJ C 59/71, 158. For e-commerce under the Brussels I Regulation, see Bonomi 2015, p. 226.

[34]Sachse 2006, p. 25; Kropholler 1978, p. 656 (no substantial-law but typical conflict of laws-protection).

[35]Case C-508/12 *Vapenik v Thurner* [2012] ECLI:EU:C:2013:790 (interpreting the EU Enforcement Order on uncontested claims with reference to the Brussels I and the Rome I Regulation). The Court made clear that there is no imbalance when both persons are engaged in commercial activities nor when both persons are not engaged in such activities [32-33].

[36]For the situation under the Brussels Convention, see Pfeiffer 2000, p. 621.

[37]Neuhaus 1976, p. 257 (dominance of the strong over the weak).

[38]Basedow 2015, p. 415, paras 626–627.

country where the consumer has his habitual residence, the contract will be governed by the chosen law but 'overwritten' by the mandatory provision of the home law of the consumer. Yet, where that level is lower, the chosen law will be applicable unrestrictedly. The process of incorporating social values into private law, its 'materialisation',[39] has thus been extended to conflict of laws, which has partly given up its traditional neutrality[40] and has overcome its lack of social values[41] in favour of goal-oriented techniques granting a party to the contract a certain substantive outcome. For the scope of consumer contracts, the formula of the precedence of conflict of laws justice over substantial justice[42] will not be applied. Goal-oriented techniques can also be found in the form of (sometimes 'hidden') conflict of laws rules in subject-specific EU legal instruments which have led to PIL fragmentation in the internal market.[43]

The substantial protection of the consumer is likewise manifest in the area of international jurisdiction. Procedural justice consideration of the interests of the creditor, the debtor, and the court. By contrast, consumer protective provisions are one-sided and attempt to spare only one party—the consumer—language problems or costs that may occur if (s)he acts under a foreign jurisdiction. In addition, although less relevant within the EU, the application of jurisdiction will influence the outcome of the case because the court of the country where the consumer is domiciled will apply the conflict of laws rules in force in that country. Consequently, there is not much room for party agreements and no place for a *favor defensoris* in consumer contract law; the interest of the competent court to establish the facts and to have easy access to evidence also takes a backseat.

---

[39]See, e.g., the works of the Lando-Group, GEDIP, SECOLA, and the Study Group on Social Justice in European Contract Law. For social justice in EU private law see, e.g., Study Group on Social Justice in European Private Law 2004, pp. 653–674; see also Collins (2011), pp. 133–166.

[40]Leible 2006, p. 366; cf., however, Id., p. 370 (criticising the principle of favourability as neither serving neither the justice of material law nor that of conflict of laws).

[41]Zweigert 1973, p. 435.

[42]Kegel and Schurig 2004, p. 131; for critique on this formula, see Juenger 1974, p. 8. For the process of materialisation, see also Sachse 2006, pp. 12–25. Dornis 2015, p. 183.

[43]Liukkunen 2012, pp. 125–126. It must be noted that under Article 23 of the Rome I Regulation, provisions of EU law which, in relation to particular matters, lay down conflict-of-law rules relating to contractual obligations, stay untouched by the Regulation. Attention should be drawn to special conflict provisions in Directives aiming at protecting the EU internal law standard by restricting a choice of law where there is a strong connection to the EU.

8.7 Congruence of Brussels I and Rome I

8.7.1 Discrepancies Reduced

The arsenal of private law to outbalance the asymmetry of information, experience, or bargaining power between the consumer and the professional is utilised on the level of EU private international law. Modern private international law is confident and does not leave it to national contract laws to provide for social justice but aims to accomplish what is known as *ius commutativa* under contract law. Therefore, the discrepancies between international civil procedure law and conflict of laws are reduced for the law of consumer contracts. Besides the rationale for protection, both Regulations share the EU market rationale under which it is recognised that foreign jurisdiction and foreign law will potentially deter the consumer from participating in the internal market. For this reason, consumer PIL contributes to the subordinated EU aim of realising the functioning of the internal market.

8.7.2 Legislative History: Blueprints

The interconnection between the consumer contracts provisions is also illuminated by their legislative history. Just as Article 13 of the Brussels Convention served as a 'blueprint'[44] for Article 5 of the Rome Convention, the definition of a consumer contract under the Brussels Convention was derived from a draft of the Rome Convention.[45] This is well-documented by the explanatory reports on the different official versions of the Brussels Convention, which hold persuasive authority due to their academic background and numerous references made to them by the Court of Justice. The Giuliano/Lagarde Report of the Rome Convention states that the definition of consumer contracts should be interpreted in light of its protective purpose and in accordance with the Brussels Convention.[46]

However, the blue-print function could no longer be sustained after the Brussels Convention was transformed into an EU Regulation, which also brought a reform of consumer protective provisions. Under the increasing participation of consumers in cross-border trade, the concept of passive consumers, who receive a specific invitation or are confronted with advertising wherefore they take necessary steps to

---

[44]Calliess 2003, p. 345; for the legislative history and different versions of the special provisions in the Brussels Convention 1968, see Hill 2008, p. 80.

[45]Nielsen 2007, Article 15, para 12; Report by Professor Dr. Peter Schlosser on the Convention of 9 October 1978 on the Association of the Kingdom of Denmark, Ireland and the United Kingdom of Great Britain and Northern Ireland to the Convention on jurisdiction and the enforcement of judgments in civil and commercial matters and to the Protocol on its interpretation by the Court of Justice [1979] OJ C 59/71, 117-118.

[46]Report on the Convention on the law applicable to contractual obligations by Giuliano and Lagarde [1980] OJ C 282/1, 23.

conclude a contract,[47] was given up. The Brussels I Regulation included all types of contracts provided that the professional directs a professional or commercial activity 'by any means.'[48] The targeting criterion was considered a sufficient link for the extension of the *forum actoris*.[49]

Consequently, the Rome Convention needed updating to keep up with its procedural counterpart and to adapt to the changes in the socio-legal environment. Article 5 was considered too narrow and national courts increasingly referred to the instrument of overriding mandatory provisions to implement substantive policies.[50] This weakened the mutual trust concept. After consulting with stakeholders, the Commission presented a Green Paper on the Rome I Regulation, which explicitly called for a transformation of the Rome Convention into an instrument of Community Law in order to both re-establish consistency with its procedural sister legal act and to pave the way for a harmonised interpretation of common legal terms.[51] This commitment was prompted by an intention to modernise consumer protection. The Green Paper mentions the protection of the weaker party as a third principle, in addition to the objectives of party autonomy and closest connection. It stressed the 'close link between the Rome Convention and the related instrument in matters of conflicts of jurisdiction' and referred to the goal of achieving consistency in Community private international law.[52] During the consultation process, the Green Paper relied on general consent to align consumer protection provisions with the 44/2001 Regulation and to ensure the synchronisation of *forum* and *ius*. The Rome I Regulation was thus adopted with the aspiration of re-establishing consistency with the related Brussels I Regulation. The draft-makers were even willing to abandon the international orientation of conflict of laws when they initially proposed copying the Rome I Regulation precisely in line with the Brussels I Regulation, which would have resulted in targeting EU consumers only.[53] After critiques, among others by the Max Planck Institute for Foreign Private International Law that a policy of 'discrimination cannot be the basis for contractual

[47]With the exception for certain contracts that involve a credit element, Article 13 of the Brussels Convention required for contract regarding the supply of goods or a contract for the supply of services, that, in the State of the consumer's domicile, the conclusion of the contract was preceded by a specific invitation addressed to him or by advertising; and that the consumer took in that State the steps necessary for the conclusion of the contract.

[48]For more on the deficits of Article 5 of the Rome Convention, Nemeth 2000, p. 46; Meškić 2008, p. 115.

[49]Proposal for a Council Regulation (EC) on jurisdiction and the recognition and enforcement of judgments in civil and commercial matters COM/99/0348 final, 11.

[50]Calliess 2003, p. 349 ('states with a relatively high level of consumer protection develop a public interest in the application of their mandatory protection regime even in international situations').

[51]Green Paper on the Conversion of the Rome Convention of 1980 on the Law Applicable to Contractual Obligations into a Community Instrument and its Modernization, COM(2002) 654 final, 16.

[52]Id., 26.

[53]Lein 2008, pp. 191–192.

justice in an international society',[54] the scope was ultimately extended to cover both EU and non-EU consumers.

8.7.3 Recitals

To some extent, the legislative history is also summarised by the preambles of the Regulations. Recital 7, the importance of which was discussed in Chap. 1, confirms the desire for a consistent interpretation.[55] Mirrored in Recital 7 of the Rome II Regulation, it explains that the substantive scope and the provisions of this Regulation should be consistent with the Brussels I and Rome II Regulations. The conciliation of the consumer provision in Rome I with the consumer rule in Brussels I is, *expressis verbis*, envisaged by the recitals of the Rome I Regulation. Recital 24 requires that the 'concept of directed activity' must be 'interpreted harmoniously' in order to preserve consistency between the Regulations. Other aims listed by the Recitals, such as legal certainty[56] or foreseeability,[57] can be more easily achieved through uniform terminology.

8.7.4 The Problem of Favor Defensoris

How should the justice rationale of protecting the persons for whom special jurisdiction is justified and those for whom it would not be realised? It was discussed earlier that the Court of Justice attempts to reconcile the need for protection of the weaker party and the commitment to avoid an extension of the scope of the protective provisions. To the extent that the protective consumer provisions are construed strictly by referring to the *favor defensoris* rationale under Brussels I, chances are that the congruence with Rome I may not be achieved in all cases. However, as explained in Chap. 3, evaluative arguments also speak in favour of not applying the *favor defensoris* rationale to interpret the consumer protective provisions. These and other protective provisions represent the legislative decision of giving more weight to the interest of the weaker party to sue (and to be sued) only where he is domiciled than to the interest of the defendant to avoid the difficulties of defending himself in the courts of a foreign country.

So far, the Court has not discovered congruence problems. Even in *Pammer & Alpenhof*, where double-derogation justified a restrictive interpretation, the Court did not hesitate to affirm a congruent understanding of the concept of 'package

[54]Comments on the European Commission's Green Paper, p. 56.

[55]See also Leible 2009, p. 43; Bitter 2008, p. 96; Lein 2008, p. 177.

[56]Recitals 16 of both Regulations; Recital 39 of the Rome I Regulation.

[57]Recitals 6, 39 of the Rome I Regulation; Recital 15 of the Brussels I Recast Regulation.

travel',[58] referring to Recital 7, which explains that the substantive scope and the provisions of the respective Regulations should be consistent. The *Emrek* conclusions may even provoke the question of whether the consumer's access to jurisdictional privilege is easier than that under conflict of laws: Recital 25 of Rome I explains that consumers should be protected only if the contract has been concluded 'as a result of' the professional's activities.[59] However, taking into account that Recital 24 calls for a consistent interpretation of the 'direct activity' condition in both Brussel I and Rome I, it seems unlikely that the Court would come to a different conclusion for the conflict of laws question. It also makes sense not to insist on the existence of a 'cause-effect' criterion and to focus on the mere existence of commercial activities that are pursued or directed in the consumer's country of domicile or residence. It is up to the national court to establish the necessary facts, in particular whether the trader has 'manifested its intention'[60] to establish such commercial relations. Consequently, the mere use of a website will not be sufficient to trigger the application of the consumer protective rules.[61] On the other hand, the actual conclusion of a contract between a trader in one country and a consumer in another country via a webpage may indicate the targeting activity of the first.[62] Although the *Emrek* case demonstrates that this activity will not always induce the consumer to leave his home country, it would be against the rationale of consumer contract provisions to let the trader benefit from the arrival of such an aleatory moment. The trader's instigation may not have been directly successful,

---

[58] Joint Cases C-585/08 *Peter Pammer v Reederei Karl Schlüter GmbH & Co. KG* and C-144/09 *Hotel Alpenhof Gesmbh v Oliver Hellerand* [2010] I-12527 [43].

[59] Saumier 2014, p. 205.

[60] Joint Cases C-585/08 *Peter Pammer v Reederei Karl Schlüter GmbH & Co. KG* and C-144/09 *Hotel Alpenhof Gesmbh v Oliver Hellerand* [2010] I-12527 [75].

[61] Id. [74]. This is in line with the joint declaration by the Council and the Commission on Article 15 of the Brussels I Regulation, anchored in Recital 24 of the Rome I Regulation. It can be seen as an attempt to correct or clarify the badly drafted Recital 13 of the Proposal for the Regulation 44/2001, according to which the *accessibility* of goods and services in another Member State constitutes an activity directed to that State (COM(1999) 348 final). For the limited authority of Recitals, see under 3.3. (Authority of Recitals).

[62] Amended proposal for a Council Regulation on jurisdiction and the recognition and enforcement of judgments in civil and commercial matters, COM/2000/0689, 7. Such understanding and (perceived) difficulties to establish the facts in the individual case led to vivid discussions about the design of the EU Regulation on geo-blocking (Regulation (EU) 2018/302). It was submitted that if the trader were obliged not to prevent access to their online interfaces based on the consumer's country of residence, then it would no longer be apparent from the website whether the trader was envisaging doing business with the consumer. However, this view disregards that the mere question whether a trader enables consumers to access the webpage and to submit an offer to buy a product will be but only one piece in the puzzle of the over-all assessment. Already the Court stressed that compliance with mandatory information set out by legislation will not constitute evidence of an intention of the trader to do business (id. [74]). The same rationale applies to other mandatory provisions traders need to respect. The directed-activity formula allows taking into account all facts of the case, including the activity of unsolicited selling by request of a consumer. In borderline cases, traders may use an entire range of options to indicate that they do not intent to direct their activities into the one or the other country.

but the fish followed the bait.[63] For exceptional cases, the criterion 'falls within the scope of such activities' will be sufficient to not unfairly subject traders to foreign jurisdiction and law.

The Court also showed willingness to construe other protective provisions of Rome I in light of the rich case law on Brussels I. When interpreting the criterion of the country in which the employee 'habitually carries out his work' under the Rome Convention, the Court acknowledged a certain horizontal harmony between the sister-Conventions and even referred to the vertical continuity effected by the Rome I Regulation, which was not applicable to that case *ratione temporis*. Most notably, the Court referred to the *favor laboratoris* principle to justify a broad interpretation of the provision.[64] It is unclear whether the Court would have paid more attention to the rule-exception relation if it had to consider the relevant concepts under Brussels I. It is also worth noting that Rome I provides for an escape clause and thus gives effect to the law of another country than that which is indicated where there is a closer connection to that country.

8.8 Conclusions

The privileges afforded to consumers under the Brussels I Recast Regulation and the Rome I Regulation are an acknowledgment that the need for protection of the weaker party is even more pressing in situations that have a cross-border dimension. Both Regulations show their tandem function to protect consumers by rules that are more beneficial than the general ones. The convergence of the respective target objectives is legislatively expressed by almost identical phrasing and situational preconditions for application and confirmed by the *travaux préparatoires*. In the realm of consumer contracts, the discrepancies between the procedural justice model under the Recast Regulation and the conflict of laws justice model under the Rome I Regulation are reduced to social values under substantial law and have been transferred into private international law. Save for exceptions, jurisdiction and applicable law can be determined by the same criteria, which will lead to a

---

[63]The approach of the proposal of the Rome I Regulation to not grant consumer protection where the professional 'did not know where the consumer had his habitual residence and this ignorance was not attributable to his negligence' was rejected by the European Parliament. An awareness test was also proposed by GEDIP. The exception for contracts for the supply of services where the services are to be supplied exclusively in a country other than that in which the consumer has his habitual residence under Article 6(4)(a) of the Rome I Regulation is therefore an anomaly, which cannot be explained by reasonable expectations of the consumer either. See, however, the reasoning in the Giuliano/Lagarde Report, 24 (the consumer 'cannot reasonably expect the law of his State of origin to be applied in derogation from the general rules'). It could, however, be explained by a particular strong connection to that state (id. at 24), which, however, could not explain the exception for package travel, see Leible 2006, p. 368.

[64]Case 29/10, *Koelzsch v. État du Grand Duchy of Luxemburg* [2011] ECR I-1595 [41, 43]; Case C-384/10 *Voogsgeerd v Navimer* [2011] ECR I-13275 [35].

synchronisation of *forum* and *ius*. A mutual transfer of the Court of Justice case law across the legal acts will be possible. Due to different concepts and the application of a *favor defensoris* principle, certain frictions nevertheless remain.

References

Basedow J (2015) The Law of Open Societies – Private Ordering and Public Regulation in the Conflict of Laws. Brill Nijhoff, The Hague

Bitter AK (2008) Auslegungszusammenhang zwischen Brüssel I-VO und Rom I-VO. IPRax 96–101

Bonomi A (2015) Jurisdiction over Consumer Contracts. In: Dickinson A, Lein E (eds) The Brussels I Regulation Recast. Oxford University Press, New York, pp 213–237

Busch C (2016) The future of pre-contractual information duties: from behavioural insights to big data. In: Twigg-Flesner C (ed) EU Consumer and Contract Law. Edward Elgar Publishing, Cheltenham, pp 221–241

Calliess G-P (2003) Coherence and Consistency in European Consumer Contract Law: a Progress Report. GLJ 4:333–371

Calliess G-P (2006) Grenzüberschreitende Verbraucherverträge. Mohr Siebeck, Tübingen

Collins H (2011) The constitutionalization of European private law as a path to social justice? In: Micklitz H (ed) The Many Concepts of Social Justice in European Private Law. Edward Elgar Publishing, Cheltenham, pp 133–166

Devenney J, Kenny M (2012) European Consumer Protection: Theory and Practice. Cambridge University Press, Cambridge

Dornis TW (2015) Die Theorie der local data: dogmatische Bruchstelle im klassischen IPR. SZIER/RSDIE 25:183–216

Garcimartín AF (2008) The Rome I-Regulation: Much ado about nothing? EuLF 2:61–79

Hill J (2008) Cross-border Consumer Contracts. Oxford University Press, Oxford

Juenger F (1974) Zum Wandels des Internationales Privatrechts. Juristische Studiengesellschaft Karlsruhe Schriftenreihe, Karlsruhe

Kegel G, Schurig K (2004) Internationales Privatrecht, 9th edn. Beck, Munich

Kronman AT (1980) Contract Law and Distributive Justice. Yale L. J. 89:472–511

Kropholler J (1978) Das kollisionsrechtliche System des Schutzes der schwächeren Vertragspartei. RabelsZ 42:634–661

Leible S (2006) Internationales Vertragsrecht, die Arbeiten an einer Rom I-Verordnung und der Europäische Vertragsgerichtsstand. IPRax 365–371

Leible S (2009) Rom I und Rom II: Neue Perspektiven im Europäischen Kollisionsrecht. Schriftenreihe des Zentrums für Europäisches Wirtschaftsrecht 173:43–78

Lein E (2008) The New Rome I/Rome II/Brussels I Synergy. YPIL 10:177–198

Liukkunen US (2012) Collision Between the Economic and the Social - What Has Private International Law Got to Do with It? In: Letto-Vanamo P, Smits J (eds) Coherence and Fragmentation in European Private Law. Verlag Dr. Otto Schmidt, Cologne, pp 125–150

Lurger B, Augenhofer S (2008) Österreichisches und Europäisches Konsumentenschutzrecht. Springer, Vienna

Mankowski P (2006) Art 5 des Vorschlags für eine Rom I-Verordnung – Revolution im Internationalen Verbrauchervertragsrecht? ZvglRWiss 105:120–163

Meškić Z (2008) Europäisches Verbraucherrecht – gemeinschaftliche vorgaben und europäische Perspektiven. Manz, Vienna

Micklitz H (2009) Jack is out of the Box – the Efficient Consumer-Shopper. In: Bärlund JC et al (eds) Festschrift T Wilhelmsson. 3-4 Tidskrift Utgiven av Juridiska Foreningen i Finland (JFT), The Law Society of Finland, Helsinki, pp 417–436

Micklitz H (2011) Introduction. In: Micklitz H (ed) The Many Concepts of Social Justice. Cheltenham/Northampton, Edward Elgar, pp 3–60

Nemeth K (2000) Kollisionsrechtlicher Verbraucherschutz in Europa. Manz, Vienna

Neuhaus PH (1976) Die Grundbegriffe des internationalen Privatrechts, 2nd edn. Mohr Siebeck, Tübingen

Nielsen PA (2007) Jurisdiction over consumer contracts. In: Magnus U, Mankowski P (eds) Brussels I Regulation: European Commentaries on Private International Law. Sellier European Law Publishers, Munich, pp 301–325

Pfeiffer T (2000) Materialisierung und Internationalisierung im Recht der Internationalen Zuständigkeit. In: Canaris W, Heldrich A (eds) 50 Jahre Bundesgerichtshof - Festgabe aus der Wissenschaft. Beck, Munich, 617–643

Plender R, Wilderspin M (2009) The European Private International Law of Obligations, 3rd edn. Sweet & Maxwell, London

Reich N (2014) Cross-Border Consumer Protection. In: Reich N et al (eds) European Consumer Law, 2nd edn. Intersentia, Cambridge, pp 285–336

Reich N (2015) Leitbilder des Europäischen Verbraucherrechts – Funktionale Differenzierung vs. zunehmende Individualisierung? In: Kohte W, Absenger N (eds) Festschrift für Arming Höland, Menschenrechte und Solidarität im internationalen Diskurs. Nomos, Baden-Baden, pp 326–345

Reich N, Micklitz H (2014) Economic Law, Consumer Interests, and EU Integration. In: Reich N et al (eds) European Consumer Law, 2nd edn. Intersentia, Cambridge, pp 1–64

Rühl G (2007) Party Autonomy in the Private International Law of Contracts: Transatlantic Convergence and Economic Efficiency. CLPE Research Paper 4:1–41

Sachse K (2006) Der Verbrauchervertrag im Internationalen Privat- und Prozessrecht, Mohr Siebeck, Tübingen

Saumier G (2014) Case Emrek: Expanding jurisdiction for consumer claims under the Brussels regime. EJCL 199–206

Schmon C (2009) Gewinnzusagen im europäischen Zivilverfahrensrecht. JAP 19:171–175

Schmon C (2018) Schrems vs Facebook: Internationale Zuständigkeit bei Forderungsabtretung. ecolex 248–249

Sibony A-L, Helleringer G (2015) EU Consumer Protection and Behavioural Sciences: Revolution or Reform? In: Alemanno A, Sibony A-L (eds) Nudge and the Law: A European Perspective. Hart Publishing, Oxford, pp 209–234

Study Group on Social Justice in European Private Law (2004) Social Justice in European Contract Law: A Manifesto. European Law Journal, 10:653–74

Tang ZS (2010) Private International Law in Consumer Contracts: A European Perspective. JPIL 6:225–248

Weatherill S (2013) EU Consumer Law and Policy, 2nd edn. Edward Elgar Publishing, Cheltenham

Zweigert K (1973) Zur Armut des IPR an sozialen Werten. RabelsZ 37: 435

Chapter 9
Appraisal

Contents

Abstract The different rationales of the rules on international jurisdiction and conflict of laws are preserved in the Brussels I Recast Regulation and the Rome I Regulation. In contrast to the desideratum of Recital 7 of the Rome I(II) Regulation, there is no automatism to uniformly construe legal terms that are common to both Regulations. Inconsistencies will occur. Nevertheless, their commonalities, complementary design, and the overarching pediment of the Area of Justice plead in favour of a systematic-teleological approach when interpreting the respective legal

C. Schmon, *The Interconnection of the EU Regulations Brussels I Recast and Rome I*, Short Studies in Private International Law,
https://doi.org/10.1007/978-94-6265-367-2_9

terms. It will be necessary in the interpretation of each individual case to ascertain whether congruence is intended and possible. In the case of consumer contracts, the discrepancies between the procedural justice model under the Brussels I Recast Regulation and the conflict of laws justice model under the Rome I Regulation are reduced. Social values under substantial law have been transferred into private international law. Save for exceptions, jurisdiction and applicable law can be determined by the same criteria, which will lead to a synchronisation of *forum* and *ius*.

Keywords Interconnection · EU Private International Law · Area of Justice · System · Characteristics · Consistency · International Jurisdiction · Conflict of Laws · Brussels I Regulation · Rome I Regulation

9.1 Brussels I and Rome I Are Complementary Instruments

9.1.1 Firm Interconnection Due to Harmonisation

The Brussels I Recast and the Rome I Regulations are companions in a gradual unification process of EU private international law. Their predecessors already had a complementary function, as the Rome Convention was created to thwart the tactical manoeuvre of forum shopping possible under the Brussels Convention. The amalgamation of PIL and EU law has led to an even firmer systematic interconnection between the Brussels I Recast and the Rome I(II) Regulations. It is significant that after the EC competence granted by Article 65 TEU was implemented, the demarcation line has increasingly been drawn between different Union instruments rather than by reference to domestic law.

Harmonisation under the same EU competence norm means to understand Brussels I and Rome I as 'Law of the European Union', which follows, and must respect, EU objectives. Doctrines of Union law, such as the duty of sincere co-operation or the principle of *effet utile*, interlink the Regulations. When designing and interpreting PIL rules, it must be considered that they require realisation of an EU Area of Justice and that they take part in the ongoing EU integration process. The creation of an ever-closer Union is witnessed by the abolition of the exequatur in the Recast Regulation. It is an additional function of EU PIL that it serves the implementation of internal market rationale. The need to judge and interpret PIL law in light of EU principles has been demonstrated within and outside the scope of Brussels I and Rome I. One may think of the four freedoms, which have shaped international corporate law, the Europeanisation of the *ordre public* doctrine, and the *Ingmar* ruling.[1] As regards the scope of Rome I, the frontal

[1]Case C-381/98 [2000] ECR I-9305.

attack of Savigny's PIL rationale in the form of EU law-protecting mandatory provisions serves as an example of the interrelation between EU law and private international law. As EU law, private international law must also respect the transnational interests of the Member States and be sensitive to the evolution of EU private law. It has a certain constitutional function in multi-level governance and must consider what can be (better) achieved at Union level.

Such examples show that PIL is open to a neo-statutist approach. Mandatory Union rules must be facilitated. The EU acquis must be protected. These are the leitmotivs of the EU legislator, which has thus recognised the function of PIL as advancing the goals of the internal market and restricting the application or outcome of national conflict of laws.[2] Unification within the EU is supposed to decrease transactions costs and ensure equal treatment of market participants, who should enjoy legal certainty in trade. The emancipation of EU PIL from 'classical' PIL is described in the programmatic recitals of both the Brussels I Recast and the Rome I Regulations, which bluntly refer to the functioning of the internal market. On more than one occasion, the EU Commission has attempted to take internal market rationale to an extreme, for example when it exploited the idea of introducing the country of origin principle into international contract law. Depending on the political circumstances, it is the mandatory or optional application of the EU trader's home law that enjoys support by the service. Certainly, such efforts not only ignore the flexibility and justice-rationale of conflict of laws but could result in two sets of 'conflict' rules for intra- and extra-EU relationships.

9.1.2 EU PIL Acts Are Reference Points for Interpretation

The numerous legal acts on judicial coordination, judicial cooperation, and private international law which have been adopted in the Area of Justice and which were given shape by EU law doctrines are reference points of interpretation.[3] The genetic affinity and complementarity of the Recast and Rome I Regulations and their coordinated implementation in the matrix of EU law serve as convincing arguments to adopt a systematic approach when dealing with legal terms common to both Regulations. This is also the opinion of the Court of Justice, which helped make early EU private international law a success. The Court exercised an interpretation detached from national legal concepts and strived for a uniform and systematic approach of interpretation of the Brussels I Recast and the Rome I Regulations. It is therefore no surprise that Recital 7 of the Rome I Regulation enthusiastically

[2] Roth 1991, p. 637.

[3] Magnus 2010, p. 28 (pointing out that the entire Corpus of Community law is to be comprehended as a comprehensive body of legislation and to be interpreted as consistently as possible); Hess 2006, p. 355 ('systematic interlocking').

explains that the substantive scope and provisions should be consistent with those of the Rome II and Brussels I Regulations. Indeed, what would be more assuring than to always call a contract a contract?

9.2 Infrastructural Commonalities and Differences

9.2.1 Similar Concepts, Different Demarcation Lines

Both Regulations deal with contractual situations in civil and commercial matters while excluding virtually the same matters from their scope of application. The term 'civil and commercial matters' bears the same meaning in both Regulations. An autonomous interpretation is required to ensure uniformity in all Member States. The contractual provisions are not completely aligned. Rome I speaks of 'contractual obligations', whereas its procedural counterpart uses the term 'matters relating to a contract'. The first presupposes the actual existence of an obligation, hence exempting pre-contractual obligations from the ambit of the Regulation. Culpa in contrahendo situations are governed by the Rome II Regulation, which, in turn, submits such claims to the *lex contractus in negotio*. Matters related to a contract are interpreted broadly, comprising situations where the existence of a contract is in question or where a party has failed to comply with a contractual obligation. This corresponds to Article 10 of the Rome I Regulation providing that both existence and validity of a contract will be determined by the law which would govern it under the Regulation if the contract were valid. Although the different phrasing makes it challenging to define a clear line of demarcation between contractual and non-contractual obligations, the contractual provisions have a common core that consists of an (alleged) obligation freely assumed by one person against another person. Neither Regulations require reciprocal duties. This finding supports a horizontal consistency between the Regulations. Where an action falls under special jurisdiction for contractual matters under Article 7(1) of the Brussels I Recast Regulation, the Rome I Regulation will likely be applicable as well.

Whilst the concepts align, the criteria for application of the contractual provisions do not entirely correspond. The 'place of performance' of the obligation is relevant for applying Article 7(1) of the Brussels I Recast Regulation, whilst Rome I considers the habitual residence of the performer relevant. The internal economy of each Regulation is an even more important factor that might make it difficult to attribute the same meaning to terms common to both legal acts. Both Regulations have a genuine internal balance and follow different demarcation lines. Rome I and II cover the entire law of obligations, contractual and non-contractual, and follow a *tertium non est datur* logic.[4] The Brussels I Recast Regulation follows

[4]Freitag 2010, pp. 169–176. For a view on the dividing line between Rome I and Rome II Regulation, see Plender and Wilderspin 2009, p. 47.

a different logic. It draws the demarcation line between contractual and non-contractual obligations internally and entrusts the default jurisdiction under Article 4 to deal with civil and commercial matters that fall neither under contractual nor non-contractual jurisdiction rules.

9.2.2 Systematic Differences

Classification problems in certain cases will be unavoidable when looking at the reason for the general default rule of Article 4. Brussels I is driven by the goal of providing access to the courts of EU Member States where there is a particular link to the forum seised. If the leitmotif of a legal act is procedural justice, as is the case of Brussels I, then it will find itself in the predicament of making a choice to the benefit of one party over the other. The Brussels I Recast Regulation follows the European continental decision of favouring the defendant. As it is difficult to defend oneself in the courts of a foreign country, his or her home forum should, save for exceptions, always be available, whilst a *forum actoris* should be limited to certain situations. Certainly, there are many possible links to the forum seised, such as the location of the subject of litigation or the important option of forum prorogation, and the domicile of the defendant is not placed on top of the pyramidical hierarchy of the Regulation. Nevertheless, the principle of protecting the defendant is a major difference from the Rome I Regulation, and its significance can be seen on several levels:[5] First, as a fallback provision, it provides for jurisdiction at the domicile of the defendant that is almost always available for all claims that are covered by the Regulation without requiring any connection between the facts of the case and the court. Second, it takes the lead in a rule-exception relationship to special grounds for jurisdiction. The general jurisdiction shall be the rule, proximity to the subject-matter the exception which applies only when there is a close connection of the court to the facts. Third, and most importantly for the question of whether there is a uniform understanding of legislative terms across the Regulations, is the design of *actor sequitur forum rei* as realising the justice model of a *favor defensoris*: the general jurisdiction is an expression of intent to give more weight to the interest of the defendant than to the claimant. Special grounds for jurisdictions, oriented towards proximity to the facts, are derogations, which according to the Court of Justice, need to be restrictively construed.

A strict interpretation, in turn, will complicate synergies with the Rome I Regulation, whose general rules do not privilege one contracting party over the other—even though the characteristic performance principle usually benefits the seller who sees his or her home law applied. The exception of subject-matter-related grounds for jurisdiction in the Brussels I Recast Regulation is instead the rule in the Rome I Regulation, which sets out rules realising the conflict of laws justice

[5] For an analysis of the *favor defensoris*, see Buchner 1998, pp. 50–54.

rationale to determine a single and appropriate law based on proximity considerations. There is no parallel feature to 'general jurisdiction' in conflict of laws, as a default rule would thwart its idea of qualification.[6] Brussels I follows proximity considerations as well; however, it seeks to balance the protection of the defendant with the availability of fact-oriented places for jurisdiction. It is striking that only the particularly close connection between litigation and the Member State under the rules for exclusive jurisdiction derogate the general rule of Article 4, whilst other close connections to the subject-matter only open the access to additional *fora*.

Whilst aspects of proximity to the subject-matter would benefit either the defendant or the claimant under a 'neutral' system of jurisdictional rules, it is the philosophy of the Brussels I Recast Regulation to give the benefit of the doubt to defendants where the situation is not positively covered by the respective provisions and to restrict a *forum actoris* to particular situations.[7] Nevertheless, and this is demonstrated by many cases before the Court of Justice, the requirement to strictly interpret the special grounds for jurisdiction does not necessarily require a strict interpretation of the concept of contractual matters. It intends to not give 'rise to an interpretation going beyond the cases envisaged by the Regulation'.[8] Therefore, it is likely that, save for borderline cases, the Court of Justice will treat 'matters relating to a contract' and 'contractual obligations' equally and interpret the concepts as requiring an (alleged) obligation freely assumed by one party against another;[9] this is also for the sake of enhancing legal certainty. As for the advantages of uniformity, it shall be recalled that special grounds for jurisdiction are formed in light of proximity of the court to the facts. It would therefore be particularly convenient for the parties, at least in most cases, to be able to predict the competent court and applicable law in contractual disputes. A clear delineation between contractual and non-contractual obligations would promote uniform decisions and reduce forum shopping.[10] After all, the promotion of legal certainty contributes to the common objective of the 'proper functioning of the internal market' (which may be one of the reasons why the *lis pendes* rule was modified by the Recast Regulation[11]). Nevertheless, due to the *favor defensoris* principle, inconsistencies in individual cases cannot be excluded.

[6] Mankowski 2005, p. 873.

[7] Buchner 1998, p. 16.

[8] Case C-464/01 *Gruber v Bay Wa AG* [2005] ECR I-439 [32].

[9] Same result: Briggs 2014, pp. 516, 263.

[10] Bitter 2008, p. 99.

[11] Dickinson 2015, p. 23, para 1.64 (noting that the freedom to conduct business in Article 16 of the Charter of Fundamental Rights may also be argued to support this approach).

9.3 De l'Esprit des Lois

9.3.1 Different Perspectives

The first obvious finding is that the Brussels I Recast Regulation is the central body of EU international procedural law. It thus thinks procedurally when it assigns jurisdiction to the courts of EU Member States and when it aims at making available a decision that can be recognised and enforced. The Rome I Regulation, by contrast, is a modern conflict of laws-instrument that specifies which law should apply to a specific legal relationship in contractual obligations. For this reason, disputes or contractual situations are approached differently.

The Brussels I Recast Regulation starts to come into play when a case is brought before a Member State's court. At this moment, parties and their roles are defined, and jurisdictional rules will tell whether the court is competent to hear the dispute. Apart from *lis pendens* situations, the court seised will only answer the question of whether it has jurisdiction, never whether another court has jurisdiction. For its application, Brussels I demands a specific link to the EU national forum seised. Its rules on jurisdiction, recognition and enforcement are characterised by the belief in the mutual trust of the Member States in their jurisdictions. By contrast, the Rome I Regulation is concerned with the delimitation of legal systems. Which of all state laws shall apply to the contractual situation? When a contract is concluded, the bilateral conflict rules will answer this question by approaching the case with the assumption that national and foreign laws are interchangeable. The parity of laws is a typical characteristic of Savignian type conflict rules, even though the Rome I Regulation has shaken off some of the classical ideals. Whilst Brussels I is based on the principle of reciprocity, Rome I is universal and, to a large extent, non-discriminatory.

9.3.2 Different Characteristics

Brussels I and Rome I have absorbed EU principles and adjusted their DNA to serve the internal market and the EU Area of Justice. However, although there are several systematic and teleological commonalities between the Regulations, there are striking differences rooted in the nature of the rules of international jurisdiction and conflict of laws, respectively.

The Brussels I Recast Regulation shows its procedural DNA in that it intertwines state interests to regulate disputes linked to its territory with the interest of the parties to have access to a court that conducts a fair proceeding. The perspective of the court is imperative as this is the entity that must issue an enforceable decision. It must also respect due process principles and consider the interest of both the creditor and the debtor to take or fight actions before a court of a country that operates within the most familiar or most convenient legal environment. Brussels I is governed by the imperative of providing effective judicial protection and, by assigning jurisdictional competence to several courts, it retains the 'serving role'[12] of procedural law. Many procedural rules are manifestations of physical control exercised by the forum country over the dispute, which must consider the effective taking of evidence, geographical distances, and procedural costs. The promotion of the free movement of judgments is another manifestation of its serving role, which will also have an impact on the interpretation of certain provisions. The sound administration of justice and access to it are features of both Brussels I Recast and Rome I. However, translated into procedural language, these objectives prevent discretionary power and command active advancement against a proliferation of competent courts in order to avoid irreconcilable decisions in different countries and to eliminate abusive litigation. Predictability and mutual trust are a greater inspiration for interpretation under the Recast Regulation than under the Rome I Regulation.

In general, the Rome I Regulation is much less concerned with questions of fair trial or issues of procedural economy. Parity, Neutrality, Universality: These are the virtues to which the Rome I Regulation wants to live up, at least partly. Even though it has shaken off some ideals of Savignian type conflict rules and has adapted to the reality of an EU internal market, Rome I is still driven by the aim of identifying the law best suited to a contractual situation. It understands proximity as the search for the closest connection of national laws with the contractual relationship.[13] It shows multilateralism in that it begins the search from the legal relationship and assigns it to a particular legal order by conflict of laws rules. It is all about the delimitation of legal systems instead of regulating a certain legal relationship when it first categorises contractual obligations and then asks for the law applicable to them. The general scheme of the Rome I Regulation therefore shows many infrastructural differences compared to the Brussels I Recast Regulation. It does not make a differentiation, as Brussels I does, according to whether one party is domiciled within or outside the European Union. Rome I Regulation does not provide a real 'fallback' provision in favour of one party to the contract. Instead, it operates with general rules for all contracts and default rules in absence of a choice of law. Typical for a conflict of laws instrument, the respective roles of the parties are not the focus of Rome I, which as a general rule follows the leitmotif of proximity to the facts; its objective connecting factors are an abstraction of the seat of the legal relationship, which yield to the law of another country where a closer connection is manifest.

[12]Pfeiffer 1995, p. 115.

[13]Von Savigny 1849, p. 28 ("daß bei jedem Rechtsverhältnis dasjenige Rechtsgebiet aufgesucht werde, welchem dieses Rechtsverhältnis seiner eigenthümlichen Natur nach angehört oder unterworfen ist"); Neuhaus 1976, p. 49. It should be noted that in this argument, Savigny was preceded by Wächter who focused on the legal relationship being a guide for the court to apply law. However, he adopted a *lex fori* approach and concluded that the court must always follow its own domestic law, see Lipstein 1981, p. 22.

9.3.3 Practicalities of International Trade and EU Focus Shift Boundaries

What is common to both Regulation is that they have the function of advancing the objectives of the internal market and creating a genuine intra-EU area of justice. Brussels creates harmonised jurisdictional rules and enables a free circulation of judgments in civil and commercial matters within the Union. Its mission is to guarantee a sound administration of justice, the navigation of concurrent proceedings and the avoidance of irreconcilable judgments. Mutual trust in the Member States' jurisdictions serves as justification to abandon corrective options, such as the exequatur procedure. The harmonised conflict rules under Rome I can be understood as flanking measures, which are supposed to lead to an EU-international harmony of decisions and thus also to avoid forum shopping. For the sake of strengthening the internal market, strict parity of laws has been foregone. Imperative EU interests are advanced by its internal market clause and overriding mandatory provisions. Another correction is formed by the *ordre public*, demonstrating that there is no value-blind formalism in conflicts of laws. There are other examples that both Regulations anchor elements of modern private international law models: Private interest-oriented rules serve the practicalities of the international market and rules protecting the weaker party to a contract supersede the idea of neutrality. Modern EU PIL rules no longer leave it to national contract laws to provide for social justice but accomplish what is known as *ius commutativa* under contract law. EU PIL is increasingly outcome-oriented and is tasked with advancing the free movement of goods and strengthening the internal market.

9.4 Party Autonomy—A Common Pillar

9.4.1 A Utilitarian Strive for Autonomy

The private interest-oriented rules on party autonomy are a good example of the common function of the Brussels I Recast and the Rome I Regulations to serve the practicalities of international trade. Their rules are exemplary of a shift from state-power-oriented to private-interest-oriented legislation. It shall be up to the parties to decide themselves on a beneficial or neutral forum or a beneficial or neutral law. Choice of law and forum selection clauses in international contracts increase economic efficiency and proper business conduct.

Accordingly, the contracting parties are free to choose the law governing their contract—to the entirety or to only part only of the contract—(Article 3 Rome I) and are free to designate their preferred court (Article 25 Brussels I). Another commonality is the declared intention of the parties as a concept that requires no particular connection between the choice made and the contractual relationship. Both Regulations put private autonomy in chains in favour of the mandatory regulation of certain subject-matters or to address public values. There are differences, too. Most importantly, party autonomy is considered the cornerstone of the Rome I Regulation. It follows a liberal approach when it grants the parties of a contract the ability to choose their law for every kind of contract and when it tends to uphold a choice of law. No reference is made to any substantial or reasonable connection between the chosen law and the contractual relationship, and the selection of any state law is permitted. The requirements are rather low in comparison to its procedural counterpart. A choice of law can also be implied by factual circumstances of the case, such as the number of connections to different laws or pre-contractual correspondence. Brussels I also attributes a strong role to party autonomy. Save for exceptions, the autonomy of the parties to a contract should be respected and rules on the *lis pendens* and enforcement ensure the effectiveness of agreements.

9.4.2 Tribute to Distinctive Nature

On a more granular level, the relevant rules pay tribute to the fundamental and distinctive characteristics of rules on jurisdiction and conflict of laws, respectively. As regards the Rome I Regulation, this is demonstrated by an exclusive and universal design and by the way it pays respect to all the circumstances of the case to determine the connecting factor of party autonomy. Rome I tends to review the result of a choice in light of public policy and other considerations but abstains from invalidating choices altogether. Its maxim is to respect the expectations of the parties, even though it shows certain discriminatory tendencies in intra-EU situations. The jurisdictional rules under the Brussels I Recast Regulation follow a procedural rationale when they provide access to certain *places* for litigation. Party autonomy thus opens the door for a variety of options, including non-exclusive or asymmetrical forum agreements. Other aspects are imprinted by procedural ideas as well: Brussels I has the predictability of litigation and procedural farness in mind when it sets out formal criteria for a choice-of-court. If choices are made contradictory to overriding principles, Brussels I tends to invalidate the choices altogether. Clear-cut rules thereby serve yet another purpose, which is procedural efficiency in the internal market. Jurisdictional conflicts should be avoided and mutual trust in the administration of justice fostered. These are the reasons why the true intention of the parties must give way in case of jurisdiction by party submission and why jurisdiction agreements are 'robust' and not open for re-evaluation other than by the court of origin.

9.5 Flexibility and Predictability

9.5.1 Fast and Hard Rules Under Brussels I

Against the backdrop of the need for uniform application of EU law, assessment of how the Regulations address the postulates of predictability on the one hand and the need of flexibility and equity on the other is of particular relevance for the interpretation of legal terms common to both Regulations. Tensions must be dissolved at the level of interpretation. Under 'legal certainty', several factors and questions may be addressed, including systematic order, realisation of party autonomy, differentiation between rules and exceptions, and firm and default rules of an exclusive or alternative nature. It may require the absence or presence of flexible mechanisms and the uniform application of rules. It may also operate at the judicial level by asking how to apply the PIL rules from the perspective of the court. From the point of view of the parties, it comes in the form of foreseeability of the competent court and the applicable law. At the level of interpretation, it concerns the construction of (ambiguous) rules.

Common to both Regulations is the provision of a framework defined by a rule-exception relationship, the priority to party autonomy, and systematisation according to objective, type-specific connection factors. Particularly due to the fact that the freedom of parties to choose the competent forum and applicable law is largely respected by both Regulations, legal certainty will regularly be achieved by an agreement between the parties. Where no agreement has been made, a closer look reveals that the Brussels I Recast Regulation has set out hard-and-fast rules, hence serving the interest of legal certainty and procedural economy. It follows the idea expressed by the Court in *Kolassa* that the rules of international jurisdiction should not be complex but readily applied by the court.[14] The Court of Justice has given much authority to the principle of legal certainty: the plaintiff should be able to identify the court before which he may bring an action whilst the defendant should be able to foresee the court before which he may be sued. There is no place for a *forum non conveniens* under Brussels I where a closer link to a court of another country exists. Member States' courts have no discretion to determine a more (or the most) appropriate forum. The tendency to give priority to clear, predictable rules over flexibility considerations is in line with the strong influence of civil law traditions on the Brussels Convention, which is characterised by a system of hierarchically-ordered grounds of jurisdiction. Once jurisdiction is established, a review can only be admissible in exceptional cases.

[14] This corresponds to the 'golden rule' of administrability and predictability of Gaimer, according to which jurisdictional law must be clear and simple. See Pfeiffer 1995, p. 221.

9.5.2 *Flexibility Answers the Need of Justice in Individual Cases*

Rome I, too, puts the focus on legal certainty. After all, the Regulation was adopted to enhance predictability of the outcome of litigation. The same national law should be designated irrespective of the (EU) country of the court in which an action is brought; parties should be able to know upon entering into a contract what law will apply. Legal certainty is also the reason why Rome I calls for a clear definition of habitual residence. Yet, typical of a conflict of laws legal act, there are many prominent options for flexibility which address the need for justice for the merit of an individual case. The system of Rome I is exemplified by the concepts of closest connection and characteristic performance, which require certain discretion by the court. The catalogue of objective connecting factors of the Rome I Regulation yields to escape rules, which are 'the inevitable counterparty of a general conflict rule intended to apply to almost all types of contracts'.[15] Flexibility in individual cases provides for international convergence. It is a typical feature of conflict rules to operate with a closest connection criterion test.

Its procedural counterpart, on the other hand, struggles with unstable connecting factors, rejects the need to find the best court to hear the case, and sees the need for procedural justice satisfied by an *a priori* assumption that the rules on jurisdiction are 'most appropriate'; derogations on the basis that there is a better court to hear the case are rejected. Instead, much authority is given to the principle of 'legal certainty', which bans exorbitant *fora* and inspires a strict interpretation of the special grounds for jurisdiction and the *lis pendens rule* in due consideration of mutual trust and the sound administration of justice within the European Union. If legitimate expectations are not respected, such as where the *lis pendens* rule is construed as prevailing party autonomy, antinomies follow. That a potential defendant should be able to know in advance the court before which he may be sued 'constitute[s] the foundation' of the jurisdictional system.[16] It can be concluded that judicial conflicts and risks of non-enforcement should be avoided and predictability of the outcome of litigation promoted. In the realm of international jurisdiction, the relevance of the principle of legal certainty has been changed from a subordinate role to a guiding principle in its own right.[17] The Court of Justice has used it in conjunction with or as justification for other aims, such as the 'strengthening of legal protection',[18] 'foreseeability of parties to identify the courts',[19] and the proper application of the *lis pendens* doctrine.[20] Furthermore, it

---

[15]Report on the Convention on the law applicable to contractual obligations by Giuliano and Lagarde [1980] OJ C 282/1, 22.

[16]Case C-464/01 *Gruber v Bay Wa AG* [2005] ECR I–439 [45].

[17]Dickinson 2007, pp. 116–136.

[18]Case C-38/81 *Effer v Kantner* [1982] ECR 825.

[19]Case C-125/92 *Mulox IBC Ltd v Hendrick Geels* [1993] ECR I-4075.

[20]Case C-116/02 Gasser v Misat [2003] ECR I-14693.

was used as a basis for interpretation.[21] The tensions between predictability and discretion can lead to situations where legal terms common to both Regulations will not be interpreted harmoniously.

9.5.3 No Principle of Closest Connection Under Brussels I

Rules on international jurisdiction acknowledge that proximity to the facts can improve the quality of legal proceedings and the sound administration of justice. It is about procedural economy, access to evidence, and respect for the interest of the parties and the court. Accordingly, the Brussels I Recast Regulation distinguishes between certain types of jurisdiction as general, special, or exclusive in nature. However, it was already mentioned that under Brussels I, only particularly close connections of protective grounds for jurisdiction derogate the general rule of Article 4, whilst other close connections only open access to additional *fora*. There is no parallel feature of an escape clause under Brussels I as the jurisdictional rules are *a priori* most appropriate. This comes at the price of injustice in certain cases.

9.6 Both Regulations Protect the Weaker Party

9.6.1 Privileges for Consumers

Both Regulations acknowledge that the need for protection of the weaker party is even more pressing in situations having a cross-border dimension. Businesses can operate their product and financing strategy under various legislations, consumers usually cannot. Consumers have no cost-justified incentive to learn about peculiarities of different jurisdictions and will often blindly agree to terms of contracts with choice of law or jurisdiction clauses. Modern private international law wants to relieve consumers from burdens through jurisdictional privileges, including language problems, lack of information, and the fear of the unknown. For a start, party autonomy is restricted. As the Green Paper of the Rome I Regulation puts it: if there are no limits to the principle of free will, consumers may well have to accept a law which is unfavourable to them.[22] As this is the case under substantive consumer law, party autonomy is considered a tool of the stronger party to enforce his power

[21]Case C-281/02 *Owusu v Jackson* [2005] ECR I-1383.

[22]Green Paper on the Conversion of the Rome Convention of 1980 on the Law Applicable to Contractual Obligations into a Community Instrument and its Modernization, COM(2002) 654 final, 10.

over the weaker party. Thus, forum selection may only grant the consumer an additional forum; a choice of law may not deprive the consumer of that level. Second, group-specific default rules ensure that consumers can rely on access to domestic courts and domestic law protection. With respect to the Rome I Regulation, the characteristic-performance approach, hence the general preference for the seller's home law, is relinquished. Under the Brussels I Recast, the privilege for defendants (Brussels I Recast) and the proximity-based grounds for jurisdictions take the back seat, save for exclusive jurisdictional grounds. The fact that the trader is "fishing" for consumers is a sufficient connection of the contract to the domicile of the consumer. The design and rationale of the consumer protective provisions show that EU private international law realises a genuine rationale of consumer protection and that it adopts a regulatory policy of implementing social values from substantial law into EU PIL. It seeks to compensate for the imbalance between parties in contracts concluded between a consumer and a professional. It seeks to protect the weaker party from exploitation whether this party is in an active or passive role and regardless of whether this party acts in the role of the defendant or claimant.

9.6.2 Synchronisation of Forum and Law Achieved

The lawmaker thus ensured that the arsenal of private law to outbalance the asymmetry of information, experience, or bargaining power between the consumer and the professional is utilised on the level of EU private international law. It ensured that the target objectives of the Brussels I Recast Regulation and the Rome I Regulation converge and designed the consumer protective provisions in harmony with each other. Thus, the discrepancies between international civil procedure law and conflict of laws are diminished for the law of consumer contracts. Identical phrasing and identical situational preconditions for applications will usually lead to a synchronisation of *forum* and *ius*.

Certain frictions, however, remain. A cause for concern is the application of a *favor defensoris* principle under the Brussels I Recast Regulation. To the extent that the protective consumer provisions are construed strictly by referring to the protection of the defendant under Brussels I, the congruence with Rome I is at stake. Notably, consumer protective provisions derogate twofold: from the jurisdictional ground for contracts and from the general ground for jurisdiction. However, a *favor defensoris* principle should not be used for exercising a blind rule-exception method. Rather, it is critical to identify the rationale of the relevant provision by using evaluative reasoning. For example, under the aspect of party interests and protection of legitimate expectations, logic dictates that a *favor defensoris* cannot apply where the defendant (expressly or 'implicitly' where the defendant enters an appearance) agrees to abandon his general jurisdiction. A strict interpretation should therefore only be exercised in as much as it is necessary to ensure that an agreement was actually made.[23] As regards the consumer protective provisions, evaluative reasoning leads to the conclusion that it was the lawmaker's intention to give more weight to the interest of the weaker party to sue (and to be sued only) where he is domiciled than to the interest of the defendant to avoid the difficulties of defending himself in the courts of a foreign country. The objective of protecting the defendant as the party to a litigation who is considered as generally having the weaker position is trumped by the objective of protecting the party to a contract who is considered as generally having the weaker position. The avoidance of a *favor actoris* should thus not be invoked to justify a particularly strict interpretation of the special grounds for jurisdiction; at least as far as the imbalance of the parties is clear.

9.7 Conclusions: No General Horizontal Consistency

It is evident that the fundamentally different rationales of rules on international jurisdiction and conflict of laws have not been abandoned but are preserved in the Regulations. Differences which relate to the Regulations' systems, their individual justice models, guiding principles, and their balance of flexibility and legal certainty have a clear impact on the level of interpretation and will prevent horizontal consistency between the Regulations. In contrast to the *desideratum* of Recital 7 of the Rome I(II) Regulation, it cannot be assumed that there is a uniform terminology across the Regulations or a joint conceptual framework. Nevertheless, Recitals, commonalities, complementary design, genetic similarities, embeddedness in the Area of Justice, and leading decisions by the Court of Justice plead in favour of a systematic-teleological approach when interpreting the respective legal terms. Even though the intention of harmony is evident in some cases and much weight may be given to overarching fundamental principles, there is no automatism to uniformly interpret legal terms that are common to both Regulations. Inconsistencies will occur. It will be for the interpretation of each individual case to ascertain whether congruence is intended, indicated, and possible without conflict and therefore whether it is appropriate to attribute an identical or similar meaning to identical or similar terms within the two legal acts.[24] As regards the protection of persons considered in a weak position, an analysis of the consumer protective provisions shows that the discrepancies between the procedural justice model under the Brussels I Recast Regulation and the conflict of laws justice model under the

[23]Case C-24/76 *Salotti v RÜWA Polstereimaschinen GmbH* [1976] ECR 1831; Case C-159/97 *Trasporti Castelletti Spedizioni International SpA v Hugo Trumpy SpA* [1999] ECR I-1517.

[24]Lüttringhaus 2011, p. 557 (no general assumption for congruence); Bitter 2008, p. 99 (case by case); Lein 2008, pp. 197–198 (no absolute consistency; no automatic transposition); Cf., however, Köck 2014, p. 194 (congruence except justified by teleological reasons); Leible 2009, p. 47 (duty to uniform interpretation where no 'particular reasons' exist which argue against it).

Rome I Regulation are reduced as social values under substantial law have been transferred into private international law. The law of international jurisdiction gives priority to social-economical values over procedural justice considerations and thus echoes the call of conflict of laws, which gave up the idea of parity of laws and neutrality in favour of those values. Save for exceptions, jurisdiction and applicable law can be determined by the same criteria, which will lead to a synchronisation of *forum* and *ius*.

References

Bitter A-C (2008) Auslegungszusammenhang zwischen Brüssel I-VO und Rom I-VO. IPRax 96–101
Briggs A (2014) Private International Law in English Courts. Oxford University Press, Oxford
Buchner B (1998) Kläger- und Beklagtenschutz im Recht der internationalen Zuständigkeit: Lösungsansätze für eine zukünftige Gerichtsstands- und Vollstreckungskonvention. Mohr Siebeck, Tübingen
Dickinson A (2007) Legal Certainty and the Brussels Convention – Too Much of a Good Thing? In: de Vareilles-Sommières P (ed) Forum Shopping in the European Judicial Area. Hart Publishing, Oxford, pp 116–136
Dickinson A (2015) Background and Introduction to the Regulation. In: Dickinson A, Lein E (eds) The Brussels I Regulation Recast. Oxford University Press, New York, pp 1–54
Freitag R (2010) Rom I, Rom II – tertium est datur im Kollisionsrecht der Schuldverhältnisse – Anmerkungen zum sachlichen Anwendungsbereich der Verordnungen Rom I und Rom I. In: Bernreuther J and others (eds) Festschrift für Ulrich Spellenberg zum 70. Geburtstag. Sellier, Munich, pp 169–176
Hess B (2006) Methoden der Rechtsfindung im Europäischen Zivilprozessrecht. IPRax 348–363
Köck M (2014) Die einheitliche Auslegung der Rom I-, Rom II- und Brüssel I-Verordnung im europäischen internationalen Privat- und Verfahrensrecht. Duncker and Humblot, Berlin
Leible S (2009) Rom I und Rom II: Neue Perspektiven im Europäischen Kollisionsrecht. Schriftenreihe des Zentrums für Europäisches Wirtschaftsrecht 173:43–78
Lein E (2008) The New Rome I/Rome II/Brussels I Synergy. YPIL 10:177–198
Lipstein K (1981) Principles of the Conflict of Laws, National and International. Martinus Nijhoff Publishers, The Hague
Lüttringhaus J (2011) Vorboten des internationalen Arbeitsrechts unter Rom I: Das bei "mobilen Arbeitsplätzen" anwendbare Recht und der Auslegungszusammenhang zwischen IPR und IZVR. IPRax 554–559
Magnus U (2010) Die Rom I-Verordnung. IPRAX, 27–44
Mankowski P (2005) Internationale Zuständigkeit und anwendbares Recht, Parallelen und Divergenzen. In: Lorenz S and others (eds) Festschrift für Andreas Heldrich zum 70. Geburtstag. Beck, Munich, pp 867–898
Neuhaus PH (1976) Die Grundbegriffe des internationalen Privatrechts, 2nd edn. Mohr Siebeck, Tübingen
Pfeiffer T (1995) Internationale Zuständigkeit und prozessuale Gerechtigkeit: Die internationale Zuständigkeit im Zivilprozess zwischen effektivem Rechtsschutz und nationaler Zuständigkeitspolitik. Klostermann, Frankfurt/Main
Plender R, Wilderspin M (2009) The European Private International Law of Obligations, 3rd edn. Sweet & Maxwell, London
Roth WH (1991) Einfluß des Europäischen Gemeinschaftsrecht auf das Internationale Privatrecht. RabelsZ 55:623–673
Von Savigny FK (1849) VIII System des heutigen Römischen Rechts. Veit, Berlin

Index

C. Schmon, *The Interconnection of the EU Regulations Brussels I Recast and Rome I*, Short Studies in Private International Law,
https://doi.org/10.1007/978-94-6265-367-2

The manufacturer's authorised representative in the EU is Springer Nature Customer Service Centre GmbH, Europaplatz 3, 69115 Heidelberg, Germany. If you have any concerns regarding our products, please contact ProductSafety@springernature.com

Printed and bound by CPI Group (UK) Ltd, Croydon, CR0 4YY
30/09/2026
02225470-0013